The Book of Certainty

The
Sufi
Doctrine
of
Faith,
Vision
and
Gnosis

The Book of Certainty

by

Abū Bakr Sirāj ad-Dīn

(Martin Lings)

The Islamic Texts Society

Golden Palm Series

This revised, expanded edition
first published in 1992 by The Islamic Texts Society
22A Brooklands Avenue, Cambridge CB2 2DQ, U.K.
Reprinted 1996

British Library Cataloguing in Publication Data
A catalogue record of this book is available from
The British Library

ISBN 0 946621 37 3 *paper*

Contents

Preface

THIS little book perhaps needs some explanation for western readers, chiefly because, in the first place, although written in English, it was not written for them: it was written at the request of one or two Egyptian friends and was subsequently translated into Arabic, without a thought at that time of its ever being published in any European language.

Our aim has been to express in the language of Sufism some of the universal truths which lie at the heart of all religions. Each chapter serves as a commentary upon some verse or verses of the Qur'ān. The book is also based on various sayings of the Prophet, and to a certain extent upon a Qur'ānic commentary attributed to Muḥyi 'd-Dīn ibn Arabī.[1] As regards other influence, the reader will notice that many points of doctrine are introduced simply with the words 'They say' or 'It is said'. These words are to be taken quite literally, for it must be remembered that a great part of Sufi teaching is unwritten and even anonymous. The same truths have been passed down from Master to disciple for generation after generation; and without the help of such oral teaching this book could never have been written.

---

1 It is published under his name by Messrs. Halaby of Cairo, but most scholars now attribute it to his great follower and commentator Qashani, and in view of the doubts as to its authorship we refer to it throughout the rest of the book, wherever it has been followed, as 'the commentary'.

Its purpose is positive, for it was written in the intention of affirming truth, not of denying error. But we will mention here that in so far as it amounts to a definition of Sufism, it may be taken indirectly as a denial of certain false ideas. For example, it will be clear to anyone who understands this book that without Sufism, Islam would be like a circumference without a centre, that the first Sufi, in all but name, is the Prophet himself, and that Sufism is therefore as old as Islam. In fact, far from being a later development, as some people maintain, Sufism was never so generally widespead, in proportion to the total number of the faithful, as it was during the life of the Prophet. The same—or rather the equivalent—is necessarily true of every other religion.

As is mentioned in the text, the Qur'ān divides the faithful into two groups: 'the foremost' and 'those of the right'. Sufism comprises the doctrine and the methods of 'the foremost'. The Path which they follow is called *ṭarīqah,* and this term is used by extension to denote a Sufi brotherhood;[2] the practices of the *ṭarīqah* are in addition, but not in opposition, to what the *sharīʿah,* the sacred Law, prescribes for every believer. Esoterism includes exoterism; failure to carry out strictly the commandments of the *sharīʿah* would amount to a disqualification for entry into one of the Sufic brotherhoods.

The Qur'ān, which is the basis of both *ṭarīqah* and *sharīʿah,* affirms continually the Transcendence of God and also His Immediate Presence, as do the sacred books of all orthodox religions; but because Sufi writers, inasmuch as the *ṭarīqah* is the way of approach to God, tend to dwell especially upon His

2 This does not of course mean that every member of a Sufi brotherhood can be called one of 'the foremost'. In order to have the possibility of being among these one must first of all be following a path, and to-day the vast majority of the members do not actually move along the *ṭarīqah* but remain stationary, not being 'travellers' (*sālikūn*). As to the term Sufi, it may not be applied, strictly speaking, to anyone who has not reached the End of the journey.

Immediate Presence, as expressed in His Names the Near, the Hearer, the Seer, it has been concluded by some that Sufism is pantheistic. This conclusion is totally false; as has been said in defence of the Red Indian against the same accusation of pantheism, it may also be said of the Sufi that 'he is nothing of a 'pantheist', nor does he imagine for one moment that God is in the world; but he knows that the world is mysteriously plunged in God.[3]

The Qur'ān says of the 'foremost' that there were many in earlier times, but that there will be few in later times. In view of this last prediction the publication of an esoteric book at a time like the present may seem indiscreet and even irregular; but one irregularity sometimes calls for another: in the modern world, which is so irregular in every respect, many believers, whatever their confession, have become sceptics and even infidels for want of finding in their religion an intellectual satisfaction. We therefore feel justified in making public one or two ideas which may afford a glimpse of the intellectual essence of all revelation.

The publication of this third edition gives us the opportunity of making some revisions and additions, not without importance, to the text of the previous editions.

ABŪ BAKR SIRĀJ AD-DĪN

---

3 Frithjof Schuon, *The Feathered Sun* (Bloomington, 1990) p.68. See also Titus Burckhardt, *An Introduction to Sufi Doctrine* (Wellingborough, 1976), chapter 3; Martin Lings, *A Sufi Saint of the Twentieth Century* (London, 1971) chapter 5.

1 The Truth of Certainty

Moses said to his household: Verily beyond all doubt I have seen a fire. I will bring you tidings of it or I will bring you a flaming brand that ye may warm yourselves. Then when he reached it he was called: Blessed is He who is in the fire and He who is about it, and Glory be to God the Lord of the worlds. Qur'ān, XXVII: 7–8.

IN EVERY esoteric doctrine there are references to three degrees of faith, and in Islamic mysticism, that is, in Sufism, these three degrees are known as the Lore of Certainty (*'ilmu 'l-yaqīn*), the Eye of Certainty (*'aynu 'l-yaqīn*) and the Truth of Certainty (*ḥaqqu 'l-yaqīn*). The difference between them is illustrated by taking the element fire to represent the Divine Truth. The lowest degree, that of the Lore of Certainty, belongs to one whose knowledge of fire comes merely from hearing it described, like those who received from Moses no more than 'tidings' of the Burning Bush. The second degree, that of the Eye of Certainty, belongs to one whose knowledge of fire comes from seeing the light of its flames, like Moses before he reached the Bush. The highest degree, that of the Truth of Certainty, belongs to one whose knowledge of fire comes from being consumed by it and thus becoming one with it, for this degree belongs only to the One. The realisation of this Oneness is here implied for Moses in that he is summoned into the

Divine Presence with which the Bush is surrounded. Entry into that presence is the equivalent of entering into the fire. *Blessed is He who is in the fire and He who is about it.*

In another chapter of the Qur'ān, also with reference to the Burning Bush, this supreme experience is confirmed by an additional symbolism:

> *And when he reached it, he was called: O Moses! Verily I am thy Lord. So take off thy two sandals. Verily thou art in the holy Valley of Tuwa.* Qur'ān, XX:11-12.[4]

When Moses reached the Burning Bush his extinction in the Truth of Certainty is represented by his taking off his sandals, that is, by removing the very basis of his apparent existence apart from the Creator in the two created worlds, Heaven and earth. Nor could he do otherwise, for the name of the valley means, according to the commentary, 'rolling up', as in the verse which describes the Last Day as:

> *The day when we shall roll up the heavens as at the rolling up of a written scroll.* Qur'ān, XXI:10.[4]

To have been divested of all 'otherness' is to have attained the degree of Universal Man (*al-insānu 'l-kāmil*), who is also called the Sufi. But strictly speaking, It cannot be considered as a degree at all, for It is no less than the Eternal and Infinite Oneness of God, the Certainty of Whose Truth effaces all except Itself. Therefore it is sometimes said that 'the Sūfi is not created',[5] since the Truth Itself is not created, and It has effaced

---

4 Since the Qur'ān is direct revelation, there can be no common measure between a translation and the original. A translation may serve to convey some of the meaning, but is of no value whatsoever for ritual purposes. The original, which has been preserved exactly as it was transmitted to the Prophet by the Archangel Gabriel, holds in Islam the central place that is held in Christianity, not by the New Testament, but by Christ himself, who is likewise 'the Word of God' (Qur'ān, III: 31, 45; IV: 171).

5 *aṣ-ṣūfi lam yukhlaq.*

in the Ṣūfī all that was created, leaving only Itself. This Identity of Universal Man with the Divine Truth is affirmed in a holy utterance (*ḥadīth qudsī*)[6] of the Truth Itself speaking through the mouth of the Prophet:

> 'My slave ceaseth not to draw nigh unto Me through devotions of free-will until I love him; and when I love him, I am the Hearing Wherewith he heareth and the Sight Wherewith he seeth and the Hand Wherewith he fighteth and the Foot Whereon he walketh.'

The same is also expressed in another utterance attributed by Sufis to the Prophet:

> ' I am Ahmad without the letter mīm. I am an Arab without the letter ʿain. Who hath seen Me, the same hath seen the Truth. [7]'

The letter *mīm* is the letter of death, that is, of ending, and the letter *ʿain* is the letter of the source of creation, that is, of beginning, and in the Truth of Certainty all that has to do with beginning and ending has been reabsorbed, leaving only That Which has neither beginning nor end, namely *aḥad*, One, and *rabbī*, my Lord. These words refer especially to that aspect of the Truth which is named Eternity after extinction (*al-baqā baʿd al-fanāʾ*), for all that is subject to change has been extinguished, and That which remains, the Eternal (*al-bāqī*), is beyond all change whatsoever. This Remainder is the Real Self, and the self which has a beginning and an end, and which corresponds to Ahmad the Arab, is only an appearance. That the Real Self is none other than God is also affirmed in yet another utterance of the Prophet:

6 A distinction must be made between the *ḥadīth qudsī* in which the Divinity speaks directly, in the first person, and the *ḥadīth sharīf* (noble utterance), in which the Prophet himself speaks in the first person as a human individual.

7 *ana aḥmadun bilā mīm; ana 'arabiyyun bilā 'ain; man ra'ānī faqad ra'ā 'l-ḥaqq.* Ahmad, like *Muḥammad* (the Glorified) of which it is the superlative form, is

'Who knoweth himself, the same knoweth his Lord'

The Self is All that is left to Universal Man in whom the veils of the self which hid It have been utterly consumed by the Truth. Thus it is said in the Chapter of the Cow:

We make no distinction between any of His Apostles.

Qur'ān, II:285.

for in the Truth of Certainty each of them is nothing but the Self, and the Self is always One and the Same; and it was because of the Self above all that the Angels were told to prostrate themselves before Universal Man in the form of Adam.[8] The Self, Which is the Truth of Certainty, is One; but It is not one with the oneness of a single thing among many, but with Oneness Which Eternally annihilates all duality, and nothing can be added to It so as to make more than One, for It is already Infinite. This Infinite Unity (*al-ahadiyyah*) is sometimes called He (*huwa*) or the Essence (*adh-dhāt*). The Garden of the Essence is therefore the Highest of all the Paradises, or rather, in the Truth of Certainty, It is the One Paradise, the Paradise of Him, and nothing may enter It since Everything is already there. Thus if it be said that one has entered the Garden of the Essence, the meaning is that his self has been reduced to nothing and that he has thus been changed from one into nought, since only nought may enter It. This knowledge of the nothingness of oneself is what is called poverty (*al-faqr*), and it is implied in the utterance of Jesus: 'It is easier for a camel to pass through the eye of a needle than for a rich man to enter the Kingdom of Heaven.' In respect of poverty one may see a fur-

---

one of the names of the Prophet. Another name is *Ṭā Hā* (see footnote on p. 58).

8 In Islam it is lack of spiritual courtesy (*adab*) to speak of a Prophet by his bare name. The original version reads 'our liege-lord Adam (our liege-lord Jesus, etc.)—Peace be on him!' But we have reluctantly decided to conform in this respect to European custom, so as to avoid unnecessary strangeness.

ther meaning in the words: 'We make no distinction between any of His Apostles', considering this time not so much the Self as the selves of the Apostles; for though it is said in the Chapter of the Night Journey:

> *And We have favoured some of the Prophets above others, and unto David we gave the Psalms.*   Qur'ān, XVII: 55.

these distinctions of favour only refer to what is below the Paradise of the Essence, whereas in the Essence Itself they are all equal in realizing the truth:

> *God is the Rich and ye are the poor.*   Qur'ān, XLVI: 38.

It is in this equality that the Prophets are rated at their highest worth; for they are incomparably greater and richer by reason of their poverty than by reason of all their earthly and heavenly plenitudes, since this nothingness and poverty is the key by which alone one may have access to the Infinite Riches of the Truth; and yet since the being is utterly extinguished in the Truth he cannot be said to have gained possession of Its Riches, for in Reality He has never ceased to possess Them.

Before extinction, the being is veiled by the Qualities[9] from the Essence, that is, by multiplicity from Unity, and at extinction he is veiled by the Essence from the Qualities, whereas in Eternity after extinction He is veiled neither by the Qualities from the Essence, nor by the Essence from the Qualities, yet the Qualities are not other than the Essence. This Greatest of all Mysteries, the Mystery of the Infinitely Rich Who is One, is expressed in the Supreme Name *Allāh* (God, the Divinity), which signifies the Essence together with all the Qualities in Indivisible Unity. In view of this Mystery it is said:

> *Say: He, God, is One, God, the Eternally Sufficient unto Himself.*   Qur'ān, CXII: 1-2.

9 Such as, for example, His Mercy, Majesty, Beauty, Strength.

Lest in the weakness of human conception the Infinite Riches contained in God should as it were overflow into duality, the Supreme Name is safeguarded between two affirmations of His Unity, 'He' signifying the Pure Essence in Itself without any differentiation as regards the Qualities. Then, to wipe away the stain of any idea of limitation or insufficiency that the human intelligence might conceive, the Name of Divinity is uttered again, and with it the Name of Absolute Plenitude, the Eternally Sufficient unto Himself (*aṣ-ṣamad*).

The Truth is One, yet Its Unity implies, for the believer, no fear of any loss, since the Truth is also the Infinitely Good (*ar-raḥmān*[10]) and the All-Bountiful (*al-karīm*). That which is taken away by extinction is restored in Eternity according to the Infinite measure of Its Real Self. The different beings are extinguished in the Truth as different colours that are reabsorbed into the principial whiteness of light. Yet as it were on the other side of the Whiteness are the True Colours, Each incomparably more distinct in the Eternal Splendour of Its Reality, as revealed in the Light of the Whiteness, than ever it was in its illusory self; and yet at the same time there is no duality, no otherness.

That Which is named the Garden of the Essence inasmuch as It is the Paradise of Him, is named Firdaws inasmuch as It is the Paradise of God. The Prophet said:

> ' *If ye ask a boon of God, ask of Him Firdaws, for it is the midmost Paradise and the highest Paradise, and from it flow forth the rivers of Paradise.* '

Here the Beloved[11] have attained to Eternity after the extinc-

---

10   This name denotes the Essential Source of Mercy, whereas its manifestation depends on the All-Merciful (*ar-raḥīm*)

11   They to whom may be applied the utterance: '...and when I love him, I am the Hearing Wherewith he heareth....'

tion, which is the Divine Station (*al-maqāmu 'l-ilāhī*), the Station of Immutability; but lest their plurality should seem to imply a plurality in God, they are, when spoken of, as it were separated from the divinity being named 'those who are brought nigh' (*al-muqarrabūn*). It is they who drink at Kawthar (Abundance), the Supreme River whence flow all others and of which the Prophet said:

> ' *There are on its banks as many cups of silver as there are stars in the firmament. Whoso drinketh thereof shall never thirst* '.

In Firdaws the nigh drink also from a Fountain which , like Kawthar, is perfumed with musk and which is named Tasnīm (Exaltation). Yet the name Tasnīm, in its expression of high-raisedness, is an understatement pregnant with significance, as is the name of the River in its expression of abundance, for Kawthar is no less than the flow of the Infinite Beatitude of the All-Holy (*al-quddūs*). Nor is it otherwise with the name of those who drink thereat in its expression of nearness, which must be measured in the light of the definition of the Nearness of God:

> *We are nearer to him (man) than his jugular vein.*
>
> Qur'ān, L:16.

To speak of the Gardens and Fountains of Paradise, as also of Its Rivers, Fruits and Consorts, is to speak the truth, whereas to speak of such blessings in this world is only a manner of speaking, for the Realities are in Firdaws, and what we see in this world are only the remote shadows of Reality.

The Divinity, Immutable and Indivisible, is the Truth besides Which all other truths cease to exist. One such relative truth is that of the religious Law, and it is said that this truth may be expressed in the words; 'I and Thou', whereas the

Truth of the Path, that is, the direct way of return towards God, may be expressed; 'I am Thou and Thou art I'. But the Truth Itself is: 'There is neither I nor Thou but only He'.[12]

Universal man realizes eternally in the Truth that he is nothing and yet that He is Everything. But such realization is beyond his human soul, and this is what is meant by the saying: 'The slave remains the slave'.[13] The slave cannot become God, since he is either the slave, as in appearance, or nothing at all, as in Reality. Universal man cannot make his human soul divine; like the souls of all other men, but with an outstanding difference of quality, it implies the illusion of an existence apart from God. It differs from them not in kind, but in what might almost be called an organic consciousness that this separate existence is in Truth no more than an illusion. There is a saying that 'Muhammad is a man, yet not as other men, but like a jewel among stones'. Albeit the soul remains the soul, just as night remains night, or else it vanishes and there is day. But though the soul of Universal Man cannot itself attain to the direct knowledge of the Truth of Certainty, yet unlike other souls it is touched in its centre by a ray of light proceeding from the sun of the Spirit of the Truth; for this perfect soul, represented in Islam by the soul of the Prophet, is none other that the Night of Power (*lailatu 'l-qadr*),[14] into which *descend the Angels and the Spirit*; and the Heart, that is, the point of this spiritual ray's contact, is as a full moon in the unclouded night of the perfect soul making it *better than a thousand months* of other nights, that is, peerless among all other souls. This Moon, from which the soul looks towards the Sun of the Spirit, is the Eye of Certainty; and its presence makes the soul at peace *until*

12 *ash-shariʿatu: anā wa anta; aṭ-ṭarīqatu: anā anta wa anta anā; al-ḥaqīqatu: lā anā wa lā anta, huwa.*

13 *al-ʿabdu yabqā 'l-ʿabd.*

14 See Qur'ān, XCVLL.

the break of dawn, until the night vanishes, until the soul together with its peace is extinguished in the Light of Reality, leaving only the Absolute Peace of Unity.

Although the existence of any perfection or indeed of anything at all apart from God is an illusion, the illusory perfections of the created Universe may none the less serve as guides and incentives to one who has not yet attained to the Truth, inasmuch as they are images of His Perfection. Of these images the highest and fullest which can be readily conceived by one who has not passed beyond the limits of this world is the human perfection itself. Moreover this perfection, unlike other earthly perfections, is a state through which the traveller (*as-sālik*) must himself pass on his way to the Truth. Therefore the religions have greatly extolled the state of human perfection, setting it up as a lamp to mark the end of the first stage of the journey, just as one might tell a man who had long lived in darkness to look at the full moon, knowing that the light of the sun would serve at first rather to blind than to guide him; and so Universal Man, whose state is the End of the journey, is represented as having two perfect natures, the perfect human nature (*an-nāsūt*) being merely a reflection or image of the Divine Nature (*al-lāhūt*), besides Which in Reality it is nothing, though to the traveller it seems nearer and more accessible. In accordance with what has already been said, the two natures might be called the perfect self and the Perfect Self, the former corresponding to Aḥmad the Arab, and the Latter being the One Lord. The perfect human nature stands as it were between the traveller and the Divine Nature, in the sense that he must acquire the one before he may rise from it to the Other; and here lies one of the interpretations of the saying that no one may meet God if he has not first met the Prophet.

Universal man with his two natures is figured in the Seal of Solomon, of which the upper and lower triangles represent respectively the Divine and the human nature. In virtue of this duality he is the mediator between Heaven and earth, and it is owing to this function that he is sometimes referred to as 'the isthmus'[15] (*al-barzakh*) as in the Chapter of the Distinct Revelation:

> *And He it is Who hath let loose the two seas, one sweet and fresh, the other salt and bitter, and hath set between them an isthmus, an impassable barrier.*   Qur'ān, XXV:53.

In His Heart alone does the sweet sea of the next world meet the salt sea of this; and by reason of this meeting his human nature itself is the noblest and best of all earthly things as is affirmed in the Chapter of the Fig:

> *Verily We created man in the fairest rectitude.*
> Qur'ān, XCV:4.

The nearness of Heaven, by reason of his presence, even causes sometimes the laws of earth to cease perceptibly, just as the moon grows pale at the approach of day; and it is at such moments that a miracle may take place, such as the changing of water into wine, or the step which leaves a print upon the rock and none upon the sand. As in the Seal of Solomon, his central function as mediator is also figured in the Cross,[16] which is another symbol of Universal Man in that the horizontal line represents the fullness of his earthly nature, whereas the vertical line represents his heavenly exaltation; and yet another of his symbols is the Crescent, for like a cup it indicates his function of receiving the Divine Grace, and at the same time, like

---

15 The isthmus, which has the same symbolic meaning as bridge, recalls the ancient Roman title of Pontifex, 'Bridgemaker' (between heaven and earth).

16 'If Christians have the sign of the Cross, Muslims have its doctrine.' This saying of the Sheikh 'Abd ar-Raḥmān 'Alaish al-Kabīr is quoted by René Guénon, *The Symbolism of the Cross* (London, 1958), chapter iii: note 2.

the horns of the bull, it indicates his majesty, his function of administering this Grace throughout the whole Universe.

> *Blessed be He Who hath made the distinct revelation unto His servant, that he might be for all the worlds a warner.*
>
> Qur'ān, XXV:1.

2 The Garden of the Spirit

And for him that feareth the High Degree of his Lord there are two gardens...And beyond these are two other gardens...Therein are two fountains gushing...Therein is fruit, and the date palm, and the pomegranate... Qur'ān, LV: 46, 62, 66, 68.

BETWEEN the degree of human perfection and that of extinction in the Divine Perfection there are said to be innumerable spiritual degrees whose multiplicity is sometimes represented by a symbolic number as is the multiplicity of the different Heavens to which they correspond. Apart from considering Universal Man in the Supreme Truth, it is possible to consider him also according to his plenitude in one of these spiritual degrees. Thus, for example, it is said that on the Night Journey, when the Prophet Muhammad was taken from Mecca to Jerusalem, and thence up through the next world to the Divine Presence, he met one other Prophet in each of the seven Heavens; for this does not mean that each of these Prophets had only reached the Heaven in which he was encountered, but that as it were below his extinction in the Truth of Certainty his Spirit is considered as presiding over that particular Heaven in view of some special characteristic.

The seven Heavens together make up one of the Paradises, which the Chapter of the All-Merciful mentions in the above-quoted verses as being of the number of four. According to he commentary,[17] the two first-mentioned of these Paradises are the gardens of the Soul and the Heart, above which is the celestial Paradise, the Garden of the Spirit, which comprises the seven Heavens, and finally the Garden of the Essence Itself.

When the Archangel Gabriel appeared to the Prophet on earth, he did so in the form of a man of the most marvellous beauty, for indeed the human eye was not created to receive any more direct manifestation of the Truth than this, nor could the earth itself have endured the unmitigated presence of any heavenly power. But on the night journey, when the zenith of the seventh Heaven had been reached, all the Prophet's possibilities had been as it were reabsorbed into his supreme spiritual plenitude which is named the Light of Muhammad (*an-nūru 'l-muhammadī*); and with the Eye of this Light he was able to look upon that which he had never seen before, and indeed his sight now demanded no less an object of perception than the full unveiled glory of the Archangel. Twice only did he behold this wonder, both times during the night journey. The first vision was just before the Light of Muhammad was reabsorbed into the Light of the Essence, that is, just before his entry into the Divine Presence. The second vision was on his emerging from the Presence, before he and the Archangel had begun their return journey in descent through the different Heavens, that is, before the two splendours had begun to diminish (just as in ascent thay had gradually increased), each in proportion to the diminishment of the other's capacity for beholding. It is the full vision which is referred to in the following verses from the Chapter of the Star; and these verses express also Universal Man's direct consciousness that absolutely nothing is independent of the Truth and that even the greatest glories of creation, for all their apparently self-sufficient brightness, are not in

17 See p.vi, note 1

Reality to be separated from the Glory of the Creator:

> *And verily he saw him at another revelation, beside the lote-tree of the uttermost boundary, whereby is the Garden of Refuge. When there enshrouded the lote-tree That Which enshroudeth, the sight wavered not, nor did it transgress. Verily he saw, of the Signs of his Lord, the Greatest*
>
> Qur'ān, LIII:13-18.

In the words of the commentator the lote-tree is 'a tree in the seventh Heaven which marketh the boundary of the Angels' knowledge. None of them knoweth what is beyond it ...It is the supreme Spirit (*ar-rūhu 'l-aʿẓam*) ... above which there is nothing but the Pure Selfhood (*al-huwiyyah*) ... He (the Prophet) was not veiled by it (the lote-tree) and its form, nor by Gabriel in the fullness of his angelhood, from the Truth (when It overflowed upon the lote-tree), and therefore He hath said: *The sight wavered not*, by turning aside and looking at other than It, *nor did it transgress*,[18] through looking at itself and being veiled by the individuality.'

The Garden of Refuge is the highest part of the Garden of the Spirit, to which, in one or more of its parts or aspects, apply also most of the other names of Paradises which are mentioned in the Qur'ān. But in respect of the Spirits of those who are brought nigh, every Paradise is virtually one of the Gardens of Firdaus and may actually become so through '*That Which enshroudeth*', as did the Garden of Refuge for the Prophet and the Archangel.

Beside the lote-tree of the uttermost boundary, that is, at the extreme verge of the created Universe, there springs the

---

18 The word 'transgress' may be understood in the light of the utterance of Rābiʿah al-ʿAdawiyyah: Thine existence is a sin wherewith no other sin can be compared (*wujūduka dhanbun lā yuqāsu bihi dhanb*).

Fountain of the Spirit, which is one of the two fountains mentioned in the opening quotation. According to the commentary it is 'the knowledge[18] of the Oneness of the Qualities'. Here the traveller has as it were the 'proof' of the doctrine of Divine Unity, for it is said that from this Paradise the Qualities appear like veils of light, behind each of which shines the Light of the Essence Itself, Which is always One and the Same. Thus the commentator further defines the Fountain of the Spirit as being 'the knowledge of contemplation' (*mushāhadah*), whereas the Fountain of the Essence is 'Knowledge of the Unity of the Essence, that is, knowledge of extinction'.

The date, which is the fruit of the Garden of the Spirit, is 'that which containeth food and enjoyment, the contemplation of the Celestial Lights and of the Manifestations of the Divine Beauty and Majesty in the Station of the Spirit; for in its Paradise the kernel of the individuality still remaineth, taking nourishment and delight therefrom'. The pomegranate, which is the fruit of the Paradise of the Essence, is described as 'that which containeth enjoyment and medicinal balm in the station of Union, in the Paradise of the Essence. It is direct consciousness of the Essence (*ash-shuhūd adh-dhātī*) through pure extinction in which there is no individuality to be fed but only unalloyed delight and the cure of the sickness of seeming to be left over (apart from the Truth) in a state of insecurity.' This is the Fruit of the Truth of Certainty, and It is still beyond one who has reached only the Garden of the Spirit. But such a one may be said to have reached something more than the Eye of Certainty, for although his individuality, that is, his self, still apppears to remain, not being utterly consumed in the Truth, he at least feels as it were the warmth of Its Flames, whereas the

19   It is significant that the word *ʿain* in Arabic has the meaning of both 'eye' and 'fountain'.

Eye of Certainty[20] sees These Flames only, being the knowledge of one who has reached the state of human perfection and no more.

20 The difference between the Eye of Certainty and the Truth corresponds exactly to the distinction made by the Taoists between the degrees of 'True Man' and 'Transcendent Man'. For a full definition of these terms see René Guénon, *The Great Triad* (Cambridge, Quinta Essentia 1991), Chapter 18.

3 The Eye of Certainty

*And when We said unto the angels: 'Make prostra-
tion before Adam', they prostrated themselves all
save Iblis…And We said:' O Adam, dwell thou
and thy wife in the Paradise….'* Qur'ān, II:34, 35.

IN ALL parts of the world, but with many differences among
different peoples as regards details, tradition tells us of an age
when man lived in a Paradise on earth. But although it is said
that there were then no signs of corruption upon the face of
earth, it may be supposed, in view of the Fall which followed,
that during this age the perfect human nature had become the
basis for gradually less and less spiritual exaltation. This is
inferred by some Sufi Shaykhs from the story of Adam and
Eve, whose successive creations are said to be a sign or a
presage, from the very beginning, of two different phases
through which mankind in general was destined to pass during
the Edenic age. The creation of Adam and his adoration by the
Angels is taken to refer to a period when man was born with
consciousness of the Self, that is, with the Truth of Certainty.
The creation of Eve thus augurs a later period when man would
be born in possession of the Eye of Certainty only, that is, in the
state of merely human perfection: in the beginning Eve was
contained in Adam as the human nature is contained in the
Divine, and her separate existence foreshadows the apparently
separate existence of the perfect human nature as an entity in

itself. Finally the loss of this perfection corresponds to the loss of the Garden of Eden, which marks the end of the Primordial Age. This interpretation of the story of Adam and Eve makes it relevant to quote a saying attributed by some to the Prophet:

> 'Before the Adam known to us God created a hundred thousand Adams.'

Between the first Adam, to whom the Angels prostrated themselves and the 'Adam known to us', that is, the Adam who fell, lay the whole Edenic period. In fact the changes which are said to have taken place in 'Adam' could not have taken place in a single being, for the Truth of Certainty is, by definition, That which cannot be lost; it is as we have already seen, for him who is veritably extinguished in It, Eternity after extinction.

In the Truth of Certainty the Eye of Certainty is nothing at all; and yet for earthly darkness it is said to be a light so splendid and satisfying that at first it might scarcely leave room for the conception of any brighter lights. This may be understood from the Qur'anic narrative of how God raised Abraham from one degree of certainty to another until he reached the Truth; but we will mention this passage in more detail later, quoting here only so much as is relevant to what has just been said about the Eye of Certainty:

> *And when he saw the moon uprising he said: 'This is my Lord.'*   Qur'ān, VI:77.

He alone whose Heart is lit with this Moon may be called the true man, for not only is it normal for man to possess the Eye of Certainty but it may be said that this third Eye is his most characteristic feature whereby he is best to be distinguished from all other earthly creatures. If the earth be likened to a windowless house, then man is a watch-tower in the house, and the Eye of the Heart[21] is as a single window in that watch-tower to which all the dwellers in the house look up for their light. Without this Eye man ceases to fulfil his essential function, having fallen from his true nature; but with this Eye he is the sole earthly receptacle of the spiritual light of which he is the dispenser among his fellow creatures, so that if he is not actually lord of the Universe, he is at least lord of this state of existence, and though he does not possess the Heavens, yet the Heavens of themselves lean down to touch the earth in him its highest point. His nature is thus made so majestic and holy that the titles of Viceregent (*khalīfah*) and Saint (*walī*, literally 'close friend of God') are given to him as well as to those above him. He also, like them, is a spiritual Master who may guide others to his state of human perfection; and for himself to rise from this state and to pass through the Heavens to extinction in the Truth he has no need of any outward Master, for with the Eye of Certainty he sees the path lying open before him along the ray of light which connects the Moon of his Heart with the Sun of the Spirit. This is the normal condition of man.

21 This term, which is here the equivalent of the Eye of Certainty, always denotes direct spiritual vision, but its meaning varies in respect of the intensity of that vision; for in the Supreme Paradise the Heart, that is, the centre of being, is no longer the Moon nor yet the Sun. These are 'worn' by the Beloved as ornaments of silver and gold; their spiritual possibilities are also represented by the green silk robes and by the 'immortal youths' which go round about them, whereas the Heart is the Essence Itself. It was evidently according to this highest sense that the Sufi Al-Ḥallāj said:

> I saw my Lord with the Eye of the Heart.
> I said: 'Who art Thou?' He answered: 'Thou'.

4 The Lore of Certainty

Then Adam received words from his Lord, Who relented towards him. Verily He is the Relenting, the Merciful. We said: 'Go fallen hence, all of you together. Yet assuredly will I send unto you a guidance, and whosoever shall follow My guidance, no fear shall come upon them, neither shall they grieve.

Qur'ān, II:37-38.

IN CONSIDERING what the religions teach, it is essential to remember that the outside world is as a reflection of the soul of man, corresponding to it in all its details. This correspondence is sometimes expressed by saying that the world is like a big man, or that man is a little world, a microcosm. It is by reason of the correspondence between these two worlds that sacred utterances which refer directly to the outside world, the macrocosm, may be interpreted as referring also to the microcosm. In fact religious teaching continually draws images from the macrocosm, for unlike the true man who sees and understands both worlds, the fallen man can only see the outer world in any distinctness of detail, his own soul being for him as a dark forest. Thus, for example, what the Qur'ān says of the infidels (*al-kāfirūn*) may be understood not only as referring to the worst human beings in the outer world but also as throwing light on the worst elements in the soul of the fallen man which have their counterpart in the outer infidels. To take another example of correspondence, which bears more directly on what has gone before, one may say that the Fountain of Immortality which springs from the centre of the Garden of Eden is the counterpart of the Eye of Certainty in the centre of the true man's soul, or rather that this Eye is itself the real Fountain of Immortality, of which the fountain in Eden is as an outward reflection; and so when it is said that Adam was driven out of the Garden of Eden, the meaning is that man in general had lost the inward Paradise of the Eye as well as the Paradise of the outer world.

The state of the outer world does not merely correspond to the general state of men's souls; it also in a sense depends on that state, since man himself is the pontiff of the outer world. Thus the corruption of man must necessarily affect the whole, and the conditions of the age which followed the Primordial Age were an outward sign that mankind in general no longer possessed the inward Paradise. But although today men are so far from the Paradise as to be almost beyond the reach of any reminder of it, the men of old were still near enough to be keenly aware of its loss; and indeed it is no exaggeration to say that most of what the ancients have left behind them is stamped more or less clearly with the consideration of how a man might return to the Paradise and become once more the true man. It was for the sake of this return that the Lore of Certainty was given to man by means of the religions, and this is the guidance which is mentioned in the above quotation.

Those who seek to follow the Path of the return (*aṭ-ṭarīqah*) are mentioned in the Chapter of the Event as *the foremost* (*as-sābiqūn*) (Qur'ān, LVI:10). Of such it is said that there are *many among the earlier generations, and few among the later generations*. Afterwards there is mention of *those of the right* of whom it is said that there are *many among the earlier generations and many among the later generations*, and this may be taken as a reference to those whose virtue it is to remain on the right side of the religious Law, in contrast with *those of the left*, who are in revolt against this Law. It is owing to the natural tendency of all earthly things towards degeneration that the proportion of those who follow the Path is much smaller in later than in earlier times.

5 The Gardens of the Heart and the Soul

And for him that feareth the High Degree of his Lord there are two gardens ...Therein are two fountains flowing ...Therein of every fruit there are two kinds...   Qur'ān, LV:46, 50, 52.

THE GARDEN OF EDEN, which for primordial man was the macrocosm, corresponds to the inward Paradise of his soul. But since his soul has in its Heart the Eye of Certainty which transcends its other elements, it may also be said to consist of two Paradises. The higher of these, the Garden of the Heart, will then correspond to Eden's innermost precinct where flows the Fountain of Immortality, while the lower, the Garden of the Soul, will correspond to the rest of the earthly garden. Together these two inward Paradises make up the degree of human perfection; and since this degree marks the first stage in the traveller's journey, it is evident that the fear spoken of as leading to these Paradises is the very fear which was said by Solomon to be the beginning of wisdom; and in the words of the commentator 'fear is one of the qualities of the soul, one of its phases, when it is lit with the Light of the Heart'.

Like the difference between the two higher Paradises, the difference between the Garden of the Heart and the Garden of the Soul is shown by the fruits which are found in each. The commentary is as follows:

'Therein of every fruit, of the delicious objects of the
perception, there are two kinds, of which the one is particular, being known and wonted, whereas the other is
universal and strange; for verily every universal idea that
the Heart perceiveth hath a particular image in the soul,
nor is there anything perceived by the soul that hath not
its archetype in the Heart.'

As regards the fountains, it will be remembered that those of
the two higher Paradises are described, not as 'flowing', like
those of the Heart and the soul, but as 'gushing'. In other words
the Fountain of the Spirit is not represented as drawing its
waters from the Garden of the Essence, but, like the Supreme
Fountain, as spouting forth of itself. This must not be taken to
imply, however, that the Spirit is in any sense independent of
the Essence, but rather that there is a break of continuity
between the Supreme Paradise and all that lies beneath It. In
view of the closeness of earthly continuity the same might be
said of every Paradise; but compared with the ultimate break of
all connections whatsoever, there is none the less a certain relative continuity between the three lower Paradises, and this is
expressed in the relationship between their fountains. Thus,
with regard to the gardens of the Heart and the Soul the verse
'there are two fountains flowing' is commented 'flowing from
the Garden of the Spirit'. Now water, in virtue of its trans-
parency and its spontaneous motion, is parallel to light as a
symbol of spiritual knowledge; and although we have already
mentioned the symbolism of light, and although we hope to
consider it more fully in a later chapter, it will perhaps be as well
to touch upon it here in so far as it may help to explain the
differences between the four fountains.

It is light itself which corresponds to the Fountain of the
Essence; the Fountain of the Garden of the Spirit, that is, the

Spirit itself, is symbolized by the sun; the Fountain of the Garden of the Heart, which according to the commentary is the eye of the 'universal perceptions', has already been identified with the Eye of Certainty, which is none other than the Fountain of Immortality, and it is symbolized by the moon; and indeed the light may well be said to 'gush' forth from the sun,[21] and then to 'flow' from it to the moon, whence it flows to various objects which in their turn, according to their aptitude, may serve to reflect it again; and any such point of contact between a ray of moonlight and a reflective object may be taken as a symbol of the Fountain of the Soul. This fountain is defined in the commentary as the eye of 'the particular perceptions', and it is in fact none other than the Lore of Certainty; for this lore is indeed the source of the true man's clear perception of the particular 'known and wonted' objects in the outer world: it is his means of understanding their true nature; for just as the Fountain of Immortality which springs in his Heart draws its waters from the Garden of the Spirit, the Fountain of the Lore of Certainty which springs in his mind draws its waters from the Garden of the Heart, so that through it he is able to refer the particular objects of perception back to their universal archetypes, and to take delight in them not merely for themselves but also in that they are the shadows or images of higher realities. It is thus the presence of this fountain in the Garden of the Soul which gives full flavour to the fruits, that is, to the particular objects perceived by the senses, by revealing them to him in the fullness of their true nature. In other words it is in virtue of this fountain that even in his perception of these particular objects he remains always conscious of the Spirit.

---

21 The distinction made between the gushing and the flowing fountains is in fact analogous to the distinction expressed in the Chapter of Jonah between the sun and the moon: *He it is Who hath made the sun a splendour and the moon a light* (Qur'ān, x:5).

The line of continuity between the Gardens of the Spirit, the Heart and the Soul, represented by the unbroken flow of water between them, is none other than the Intellect. But the pure Intellect may not be said to descend lower than the Garden of the Heart. As to the waters which flow between the two lowest fountains, they represent those intellectual faculties in which the Intellect has become partially veiled by the psychic substance. These are the faculties of intellectual intuition, and they are the mediators between the reason which rules the soul and the pure Intellect which rules the Heart, their knowledge being more certain than that of the Lore, but less certain than that of the Eye. They may also be called the heavenly desires, since they are turned in spontaneous inclination towards the next world just as the desires in the ordinary meaning are turned towards this world.

In one sense these intermediary waters form part of the Garden of the Soul which is in fact incomplete without them, depending upon them for its fountain which is its most essential feature. It is thus made up of two kinds of elements, of intuitive faculties which are turned in desire towards the Garden of the Heart and which are perpetually satisfied by the light that comes from it, and of earthly desires which are turned towards the particular objects of perception in the outer world, and which are ready to be satisfied according to the possibilities afforded by outward conditions. It is in fact this readiness to be satisfied, this full development, and not the actual satisfaction itself, which distinguishes the soul of the true man from that of the fallen man. Indeed, it may be that the earthly desires are only satisfied within certain limitations.[23] But this does not

23 The Garden of the Soul depends for its full realization on the perfection of the fruits as well as on that of the fountain, so that in a sense it is only possible for the true man to possess fully the Garden of the Soul during his life if he is living in the Garden of Eden, that is, during the Primordial Age. Otherwise this Paradise

apply to the heavenly leanings of the intuitive faculties; and still less does it apply to the Garden of the Heart itself, which is above all earthly conditions, being even above death, as the name of its fountain shows.

---

may only be enjoyed to the full after death, when the perfect soul is said to abide in a prolongation of the earthly state which is, like itself, incorporeal and not subject to decay, retaining always its primordial perfection. The term 'Garden of the Soul' is in fact usually taken to refer to such a prolongation of the human state after death.

6 The Fall

*Then Satan whispered unto him and said: 'O Adam,
shall I show thee the Tree of Immortality and a kingdom that fadeth not away?'*   Qur'ān, XX:120.

IN THE CENTRE of the Garden of Eden there is said to be not
only a fountain but also a tree, at whose foot the fountain flows.
This is the Tree of Immortality, and it is an outward image of
the inward Tree of Immortality which grows in the Garden of
the Heart, bearing as its fruits the universal and strange objects
of perception. These are the objects of the perception of the
Eye of Certainty, which is the Fountain of the Heart. Until the
traveller has actually reached this fountain and the tree which is
inseparable from it, he cannot be called the true man, nor can he
be said to have safely finished the first part of his journey, for
there is always the danger that he may still be swept back upon
the general tide of degeneration and corruption which is per-
sonified by the devil himself. But once the traveller has drunk
of the waters of the fountain and eaten of the fruit of the tree,
and has thus gained the wisdom of the Eye of the Heart, which
consists in direct contact with the Spirit, he is at last safe from
all attacks of the devil and proof against all the powers of deception, this degree—that of the true man—being none other than
the degree of the true slave of God:

Verily over my slaves thou, Satan, hast no power.
                                    Qur'ān, XVII:65.

In considering therefore how Satan ever came to corrupt man, it may be concluded that at the time of the Fall, mankind in general, far from having actual knowledge of the Truth of Certainty, had begun to be born even without the knowledge of the Eye of Certainty, that is, without immediate access to the Tree and the Fountain of Immortality. Otherwise they could never have been deceived; and it is in fact clear from the above opening quotation that the Adam who fell had never seen the real Tree of Immortality. It would seem, then, that the perfection of mankind at the very end of the Primordial age was as it were a hereditary perfection, in that men continued to be born with primordial harmony in their souls after the cause of that harmony, the Eye of the Heart, had ceased to be theirs; and thus it may be imagined that the different psychic elements were still in their rightful places simply because there was as yet no actual reason for perversion, the faculties of particular earthly perception and desire remaining in the outer part of the soul, and the intuitive faculties which are the heavenly desires remaining near the centre in hopes of a vision of the Tree of Immortality. It is to these innermost faculties that the speech of Satan is addressed, since of all the soul's elements it is they alone which, from their abode at the boundary between the two Paradises, have leanings towards the universal and strange fruits of immortality and the kingdom of the next world that does not fade; and since he had in reality only the fruits of the Garden of the Soul to offer them, that is, the known and wonted objects of perception, being himself everlastingly barred from the Garden of the Heart, he could only tempt them with forgeries, giving the known and wonted objects of perception a semblance of strangeness by suggesting abnormal and irregular uses for them. Thus all his deception of mankind throughout the ages is summed up in the above verse; he ceaselessly promises to show man the Tree of Immortality, gradually

reducing by this means the highest and most central faculties
into the outer part of the soul so that he may imprison them
there in attachment to the counterfeit objects which he has
forged for their perception. It is the presence here of these perverted faculties, either in discontent in that they can never find
real satisfaction or finally in a state of atrophy in that they are
never put to their proper use, which causes all the disorder and
obstruction in the soul of the fallen man, and which is mentioned in the Chapter of the Declining Day:

> *By the declining day, verily mankind is in ruinous loss,*
> *except they that believe and do good works, and exhort one*
> *another unto truth and unto patience.*   Qur'ān, CIII.

It is significant that the Qur'ān swears to this ruin by the
declining day, that is, the time of day which comes immediately
before the setting of the sun and which corresponds to the present age[24] in which man's intuitive faculties have reached their

---

24 According to the Hindus, and also the ancient Greeks and Romans, each
great cycle of time is divided into four ages, to which the Romans gave the name
of Golden, Silver, Bronze and Iron, each age being spiritually inferior to the one
which preceded it. The end of the Primordial Age (which is beyond the cycle)
corresponds to the Fall, and the beginning of the Golden Age to the Relenting of
God towards Adam. The end of the Iron Age, that is, the present age, which the
Hindus call the Dark Age, is marked by the overthrow of the Antichrist by Christ
at his second coming. As regards the intervening period, however, the
correspondences are less obvious: the Hindu perspective is objective and
historical, whereas the Islamic perspective is subjective and 'practical'. Instead of
considering the great divisions of the cycle, the Qur'ān only mentions those few
civilizations which were known to the Arabs by name. Moreover little or no
distinction is made between the qualities of the different civilizations; the
attention is always concentrated on the fact that after flourishing for a time each
one of them came to ruin. For the Muslim, history is chiefly of value as evidence
of the perishability of all earthly things.

The Hindu doctrine states that there are many great cycles, each one being
made up of four ages; thus the end of the Dark Age is followed by a new Golden
Age. According to the Jewish, Christian and Islamic perspectives, which consider

uttermost perversion. Moreover, since it is possible, as has already been explained, to apply what is said directly of the macrocosm to the microcosm also, this oath may be taken as a testification not merely to the ruin of man as a whole but also to . the ruin of these particular faculties in man, since it is they in the microcosm which correspond precisely to the human race in the macrocosm. In the same way the following verses of the Chapter of the Fig:

> *Verily We created man in the fairest rectitude. Then cast We*
> *him down to be the lowest of the low.*   Qur'ān, XCV:4-5.

may be taken as referring to these faculties as well as to man himself. For just as man who was the highest of all earthly things becomes in his degeneration the lowest, so these faculties which were the most precious elements in his soul become the source of all its subsequent disorder, illustrating like man himself the truth which is expressed in the Latin proverb *corruptio optimi pessima*, the best when corrupted becometh the worst. Meanwhile, apart from the obstruction caused in the soul by the misplaced intuitions, the faculties of earthly perception and desire are also affected in themselves; for the intuitive faculties were as channels by which the Fountain of the Lore of Certainty drew its waters from the Paradise of the Heart, and if the channels are corrupted the fountain itself is also necessarily corrupted. The particular desires cannot grow to fullness in

---

time almost exclusively in its ruinous aspect, the whole span of the earth's existence is compressed into one cycle, so that the final ruin at the end of the present age is usually identified with the final ruin at the end of the world. But the tradition is strong, none the less, in these three latest religions, that the Messiah at his coming will rule for a certain time over the whole earth as king; and this is in accordance with the Hindu belief that Kalki (he who rides on the white horse), whose coming marks the end of the present Dark Age, will inaugurate a new Golden Age.

that the particular objects of perception are desired only for themselves, being no longer prized as reflections of universal truths. At the same time, since unlike the heavenly desires these earthly desires do at least receive a certain satisfaction, they take on an undue importance, seeking to usurp the central place;[25] and with regard to the traveller's return, it will easily be understood that one of the purposes of fasting and of asceticism in general is to frighten these desires from this usurped position. Indeed, 'fear is the beginning of wisdom', and the task of restoring order to the soul begins with the instilling of fear into the earthly desires, since it is they which immediately confront the traveller, the perverted intuitions being usually too remote from the centre of consciousness or too sunken in atrophy for him to be fully aware of their presence at first. It is only by exception that they are not definitely lost, as they are for the vast majority of the men of this age, in whom the plight of these higher faculties, analogous to that of mankind in general, is described in the Chapter of Yā Sīn:

> *Verily We have put shackles upon their necks even up to their chins, so that they are stiff-necked; and before them We have placed a barrier and behind them a barrier, and We have blindfolded them so that they see not. Alike is it to them whether thou warnest them or not, for they will not believe.*
> Qur'ān, XXXVI:8-10.

Rare indeed are those who have these faculties sufficiently unperverted for there to be the least flow of the Fountain of the Lore of Certainty in their souls, this degree of certainty being none other than that faith (*īmān*) which is referred to in the Chapter of the Inner Rooms:

---

25 Speaking of earthly desires, a Sheikh has said: 'The spiritual man *has* desires; the profane man *is* his desires.'

The Arabs say: We believe. Say thou: Ye believe not. Say rather: 'We have submitted',[26] for faith hath not entered your hearts.   Qur'ān, XLIX:14.

The believers are also referred to in the Chapter of the Declining Day, and the Lore of Certainty is the truth to which they exhort each other. But such belief by itself is not enough, and it is by a still greater exception that one may be born who not merely recognizes this truth but is actually drawn towards it, seeking to follow it in patience by 'good works' which are 'the devotions of free will' mentioned in an already quoted utterance of the Prophet. Only one who follows this path may be called a traveller (*sālik*); and the scarcity of such, even compared with the scarcity of the believers who recognize the truth, is affirmed in the commentary which says with regard to patience: 'Verily it is easy to attain unto the truth, yet as for constancy unto it and patience with it through unerring perseverance in worship, these are rarer than the red sulphur and the white raven.'

This rare virtue is none other than what is sometimes called excellence (*iḥsān*);[27] it implies the hope of regaining all that man has lost throughout the ages, and without it the traveller could never even begin his task through seeking by means of fear to make room in the centre of his soul for the return of the heavenly desires. But with *iḥsān* he will have patience to attempt this, and also patience to seek by the same means to detach these desires from the counterfeits of spiritual truth which have been forged for them in the outer part of his soul; and sooner or later he must pass through a phase complementary to that of fear, and this is the phase of love, since it is through spiritual

26 *aslamnā*, that is, we have made submission (*islām*) to God.

27 For a fuller definition of this term, and also of the terms *īmān* and *islām*, see Frithjof Schuon, *Sufism, Veil and Quintessence* (Bloomington, Indiana 1981), pp. 129-30.

love alone that the heavenly desires may actually be recalled to the centre of the soul, there as it were to await the opening of the Eye of the Heart. Moreover, this second phase may also serve indirectly the purpose of the first, since it is said that with the return of these higher desires to the centre the earthly desires retire[28] as if of their own accord into the outer part of the soul. These two phases may be more or less distinct or simultaneous, though in general that of fear precedes the other. But however they may take place, varying from one soul to another in accordance with the saying that there are as many different paths to the truth as there are souls of men, it is at least certain that until both phases be complete, that is, until the true hierarchy be entirely restored to the soul, every element having been brought back to its proper place, the state of human perfection with its two Paradises cannot be regained.

28 Very relevant to this is the saying of an Arab dervish, 'It is not I who have left the world; it is the world which has left me', quoted by Frithjof Schuon, *The Transcendent Unity of Religions* (London, 1952), p.74 note.

7 The Symbol

Seest thou not how God citeth a symbol: 'A good word is as good as a good tree, its root set firm and its branches in heaven, giving its fruit at every season by the leave of its Lord'? God citeth symbols for men that they may remember. Qur'ān, XIV:24-25.

THE ETERNAL (*al-bāqī*) is the All-Embracing (*al-muḥīṭ*): He is not only as it were after all time but also before all time, being the Ancient of Days (*al-qadīm*); and so the journey to extinction in the Truth of Certainty is likened to an act of remembrance. The same applies by analogy to the attainment of the lesser spiritual degrees, for each degree embraces or envelops the degrees which are below it. Thus time itself, which belongs to the lowest degree of all, that of earthly existence, is enveloped by all that lies above, so that the next world in its entirety, with all its spiritual degrees, is before time as well as after it; and this is expressed in an utterance of the Prophet referring to the creation of Adam's body which is at the beginning of time, and to his own prophethood which is of the next world: 'I was a Prophet while Adam was still betwixt water and clay.' It can thus be said that man has behind him not only a historical and 'horizontal' past but also a spiritual and 'vertical' past. A merely theoretic doctrinal knowledge is a horizontal remembrance: we remember what we have been taught in time; and apart from lessons in the narrower sense, the facts of the horizontal plane, that is, of this world, when looked at objectively, without prejudice, make us inclined to believe what the doctrine teaches us about the world beyond. But insofar as there is any certainty in this belief, a vertical element has been added to the horizontal; we are only certain about something because we have seen it to be true. Thus, even if we are unaware of it, the least particle of certainty that can be had about the next world must necessarily have come down from above; it does not belong to horizontal remembrance but to vertical remembrance which is nothing other than intellectual intuition or—what in a sense amounts to the same—spiritual love. We can thus add to what was said about love in the last chapter that the initial act of this way is to awaken, in the erring faculties of intuition, the vertical remembrance which is theirs by rights and which alone can draw them from the outer part of the soul to its centre, where the vertical is to be found in all its fullness, that is, in the Tree of Immortality. It is such remembrance[29] that is meant by the Arabic world *dhikr*, the general name given in Islam to all the different means of reminding man of his original state; and in every *dhikr* it is a symbol which is used to prompt the memory.

It has already been mentioned that the outer world of earthly existence corresponds in all its details to the inner world of man's soul, and that there is a similar correspondence between the Garden of the Heart and the Garden of the Soul; but these are only two particular instances of the general truth that all the different domains in the Universe correspond to each other in that each is an image of the Universe itself. The ancient sciences sprung from a knowledge of these correspondences, which was one of man's original endowments. For example, the sciences of medicine were based on a knowledge of the correspondences or likenesses between the domain of the body and

29 This recalls the words of Jesus at the institution of the rite of the bread and wine: 'Do this in memory of me.' For his body, represented by the bread, is the fruit of the Tree of Immortality, just as his blood, represented by the wine, is the water of the Fountain.

other earthly domains such as those of plants and minerals. But the work of the spiritual path does not necessarily call for a knowledge of cosmic or 'horizontal' likenesses such as these; when, in connection with the *dhikr*, the Qur'ān speaks of the *mathal*—'example' or 'symbol'—it is referring to the essential or 'vertical' likenesses between higher and lower domains, such as those already mentioned between the Heart and the soul. A symbol is something in a lower 'known and wonted' domain which the traveller considers not only for its own sake but also and above all in order to have an intuitive glimpse of the 'universal and strange' reality which corresponds to it in each of the hidden higher domains. Symbols are in fact none other than the illusory perfections of creation which have already been referred to as being guides and incentives to the traveller upon his journey, and they have power to remind him of their counterparts in higher worlds not through merely incidental resemblance but because they are actually related to them in the way that a shadow is related to the object which casts it. There is not the least thing in existence which is not such a shadow, as is implied in the Chapter of the Cow:

> *Verily God disdaineth not to cite as symbol even a gnat or something smaller.*   Qur'ān, II:20.

Nor is there anything which is any more than a shadow. Indeed, if a world did not cast down shadows from above, the worlds below it would at once vanish altogether, since each world in creation is no more that a tissue of shadows entirely dependent on the archetypes in the world above. Thus the foremost and truest fact about any form is that it is a symbol, so that when contemplating something in order to be reminded of its higher realities the traveller is considering that thing in its universal aspect which alone explains its existence.

Thanks to the true relationship between this world and the next, the 'known and wonted' objects have always, for the spiritual man, something of the marvellously 'strange'. Inversely, the Qur'ān tells us that the higher realities have, for the blessed souls in Paradise, something of the 'known and wonted', inasmuch as those souls have had experience, on earth, of the shadows of the realities:

> *Whensoever they are given to eat of the fruits of the garden, they say: 'This is that which was given us aforetime; and it was given them in a likeness thereof.*　　Qur'ān, II:25.

What is true of earthly objects applies also to acts: an earthly act is the last of a hierarchy of corresponding shadows which spans the whole Universe. Figuratively speaking, if each series of corresponding shadows or reflections throughout the different worlds be likened to the series of the rungs of a ladder, an earthly act is as the lowest rung, or rather as the support upon which rests the foot of the ladder, and to stand at the foot in upward aspiration is precisely what constitutes an act of remembrance in the sense of the word *dhikr*. The traveller may thus sanctify all his acts[30] in seeking to remember, through them, the Divine Qualities in which they are rooted. The fundamental acts of life which were given to man at his creation are as it were the primordial rites; but in view of human decadence Providence has added to these the rites revealed to the Prophets which are rites in the strict sense of the term. Each of these is as

30 The intention to ritualize all one's actions necessarily means avoiding those actions which are too remote from the Truth to serve as reminders of it. For example, murder is in itself, that is, as an act of slaying, the shadow of a Reality. It is this Reality, expressed by His Name the Slayer (*al-mumīt*), which makes possible the ritual sacrifice of an animal. But in Truth the Slayer is not to be separated from His other Names, whereas murder, unlike sacrifice, constitutes a kind of separation, reflecting nothing of the Divine Mercy, Benevolence and Serenity; the murderer is thus only a very indistinct and fragmentary shadow of the Slayer.

the foot of a ladder which the Divine Mercy has let down into the world as a vehicle of Grace and, in the upward direction, as an eminent means of remembrance. Such is the ladder which appeared in a dream to Jacob, who saw it stretching from Heaven to earth with Angels going up and down upon it; and it is also 'the straight path' (aṣ-ṣirāṭu 'l-mustaqīm), for indeed the way of religion is none other than the way of creation itself retraced from its end back to its Beginning.

The ladder as a symbol of the true rite and all that this rite implies recalls the tree which is mentioned in the opening quotation as a symbol of the good word; for indeed the best example of a good word is a Divine Name uttered as a *dhikr* in upward aspiration towards the Truth. The firm-set root of the tree is the *dhikr* itself uttered with firm-set purpose; the Heaven-reaching branches represent the tremendous impact of the *dhikr* as it passes upwards throughout the whole Universe; and the fruit of the tree is the Reality in Whose memory the *dhikr* is performed.

The images of the tree and the ladder may help to explain why the Revealed Books, which have been sent down directly from Heaven, necessarily admit of several different interpretations. These are in no sense contradictory, each being right at its own level.[30] Ranged in hierarchy like the rungs of a ladder, they are what might be called the vertical dimension of the Book in question. This dimension is in the nature of things: like a star that falls from the sky, every Revelation leaves behind it a

31 In general only one interpretation of what is quoted from the Qur'ān is given here, the one most in conformity with this book's perspective. But it goes without saying that this interpretation is not exclusive of others.

As an example of different levels of interpretation, let us consider the story of the three messengers who were sent to a city to preach there the Truth (Qur'ān XXVI, 13-29). According to the literal historical meaning, the city is Antioch and the messengers are Peter and two others of the companions of Jesus. Also macrocosmic, but higher in virtue of its universality, is the interpretation according to which the city represents mankind, whereas the three messengers luminous trail of higher truths. A profane book, on the contrary, has only one meaning and therefore no vertical dimension at all.

> *A bad word is as a bad tree which lies uprooted on the surface*
> *of the earth.*   Qur'ān, XIV:26.

---

are Moses, Jesus and Muhammad. Higher still is the microcosmic interpretation—that of our commentator: the city is the human soul, its inhabitants the different psychic elements, and the three messengers the Heart, the Spirit and the Intellect.

8 The Four Worlds

The seven Heavens and the earth extol Him, and all that is therein, and there is naught that hymneth not his praise, yet ye understand not their praising.

Qur'ān, XVII:44.

THE NUMBER of the worlds is in reality beyond all reckoning; but for the human being there appear to be four main divisions in the hierarchy, so that it is often said that there are four worlds.[32] The lowest of these, the material world is named the World of the Kingdom (*'ālamu 'l-mulk*); next above it is the world of psychic powers which is the World of the Dominion (*'ālamu 'l-malakūt*); the third, which includes all the different Heavens, is the World of the Domination (*'ālamu 'l-jabarūt*); and the Highest is the World of the Sovereign Power (*'ālamu 'l-'izzah*), Which is also the World of the Unmanifest (*'ālamu 'l-ghaib*). The first two of these really make up one world in the ordinary sense of the word, namely the state of human existence, whereas the third contains in itself many different worlds, those of the different Heavens. Similarly, if one considers the microcosm, the first two will be the world of the body and the world of the soul which together make up the human being itself, and which correspond in the true man to the Garden of the Soul. The Garden of the Heart thus lies as it

---

32 The four worlds are mentioned also in the Jewish Qabbala. The three worlds mentioned in the Hindu doctrine correspond to the three lowest of these, beyond which lies the Unmanifest (see René Guénon, *Man and his becoming according to the Vedānta* (London, 1945), p.56, note 2).

were between the World of the Dominion and the World of the Domination which is itself the Garden of the Spirit. As to the Highest World, It is the Divinity itself, apart from Which there is nothing at all, and of Which the other three worlds are as a series of reflections growing less and less distinct. It is this reflecting of the One Reality which is the praise referred to in the opening quotation, since to act as symbol or reminder of Him is all the praise of which a creature is capable; and since there is nothing, even in the lowest world, which is not a symbol and which is not above all a symbol of Him in that it must ultimately be traced back to Him as its Original, there is absolutely nothing which does not praise Him. Thus praise may be called the very root of existence, since without it a creature would fade into nothing; but the fallen man does not understand this, tending to consider earthly things as if they were independent realities, because the Fountain of the Lore of Certainty does not flow freely enough in his mind to make him conscious of their highest and most essential aspect, wherein they never cease to praise.

In contrast with the World of Reality, the three lower worlds may be considered all together as one world which may be named the World of Symbols; but this name applies especially to the material world, the World of the Kingdom, which is the most familiar and accessible, and which contains the symbols not only of the Highest World but also of the intermediary worlds.

9 The Waters

*And He it is Who created the Heavens and the
earth in six days, and His Throne was upon the
water.*   Qur'ān, XI:7.

THE FOUNTAIN in the centre of a Paradise may be said to represent the pure original substance from which the Paradise
came into existence and from which it still continues to draw its
existence. But if the pure substance be considered in itself as it
was before the Paradise was actually created, it will not be represented by water in the form of a fountain flowing amidst
already created objects, but by water in the form of a sea which
contains in itself the undifferentiated seeds of the world in
question. If this distinction be transposed to the level of the
Essence Itself, Which is above all phases of creation, remaining
Eternally as It is, one may say that the fountains are reflections
of the Essence in so far as it is the Source of all things, whereas
the seas reflect It for Its Infinity (*al-ʿaẓamah*) and for Its Eternal
Self-Sufficiency (*aṣ-ṣamadiyyah*). Of earthly waters it is especially the ocean which reflects this Aspect of the Truth, and in
Arabic the ocean is called the all-embracing (*al-muḥīṭ*) because
it is a reminder above all of Him Who is in Reality the All-
Embracing. As regards the opening verse, however, it is not the
water but the Throne which may be identified with the All-
Embracing, or at least with that Aspect Which embraces all created things; the water here referred to is the pure original substance of creation which contained in its undivided unity the

seeds of the three created worlds and all that they contain. This same water is also mentioned in the Old Testament where it is said, in the account of the creation: 'The Spirit of God moved upon the face of the waters.' Later it is said: 'And he divided the waters.' Similarly in the Qur'ān it is said:

> *Have not the infidels seen that the Heavens and the earth were of one piece? Then We rifted them asunder, and from the water We made every living thing.* Qur'ān, XXI:30.

This division is the origin of the two seas already spoken of, which are so often mentioned in the Qur'ān. The sweet sea of the Heavens is the World of the Domination, the World of the Spirit. These upper waters are symbolized especially by rain-clouds which let fall their life-giving contents upon the earth because the World of the Spirit, which they reflect, lets fall its blessing upon this world. It is in view of this symbolism that the power of rain as a remembrancer is referred to in the Chapter of the Distinct Revelation:

> *And We have sent down from Heaven pure water, that therewith We may quicken a dead land, and that thereof We may give drink to Our creatures, to cattle and men in plenty; and verily We have given of it freely unto them that they might remember.* Qur'ān, XXV:48-50.

The salt sea is this world, that is, the World of the Dominion in which the World of the Kingdom is included, or, in respect of the microcosm, the world of the soul in which the body is included, and so it is said that the pure, original substance of man was water:[33]

33 It is also said: *He hath created man from clay* (Qur'ān, LV:14), the element earth, in so far as it symbolizes elemental purity, being parallel to water. In fact, in the rites of ablution, water may sometimes be replaced by earth. As to the differences in meaning between these two elements, it may be said that earth derives its firmness and solidity from the Aspect of Eternity in the Essence, whereas water is to be traced rather to the Aspect of Infinity.

And He it is Who from water hath created man.

Qur'ān, XXV:54.

Thus in rites of ablution, the element water, with which the performer of the rite as it were identifies himself, may be taken to represent the original purity of the human nature as it was created, so that the rite is a reminder of the state of human perfection. At the same time it represents identification with the pure blessing which is the essence of the sweet sea of the upper waters. Above this it represents identification with the substance of the whole created Universe; and above all it represents the Supreme Identity, the drowning or extinction of the being in the waters of the Infinite Oneness of the Truth. These are indeed the Real Waters, and the earthly element is only a remote shadow of Water. Moreover it should not be thought that the element was chosen by man to symbolize What it symbolizes because it purifies and because it quenches thirst; the truth is the inverse of this, namely that it quenches thirst and purifies because, independently of any human choice, it is and always has been a symbol of the Pure Essence which satisfies Eternally the thirst of all desires. As such the element has in itself the active power of a remembrancer for man, to some extent even without any conscious intention on his part.

10 The Creator of the Pairs

Glory be to Him Who hath created all the pairs, of what groweth from the earth, and of themselves, and of what they know not.   Qur'ān, XXXVI:36.

APART FROM the symbolism of each separate thing as a created unit there is also a double symbolism to be considered, the symbolism of pairs, that is, of two things or aspects which are complements of each other, the one being relatively masculine and active and the other relatively feminine and passive. Now since the creation is the result of the Truth's allowing Its Aspects to be reflected in the waters of the Universe, the words: 'Glory be to Him Who hath created all the pairs' must be taken as referring to the Creator in that particular aspect of Which the pairs are reflections. In other words, the reference is to the One who is not only the Majestic (*al-jalīl*) but also the Beautiful (*al-jamīl*), the One Who has not only Infinite Riches to give but also Infinite Capacity to receive. According to this Aspect of the Truth, some of His Qualities are termed the Qualities of Majesty (*aṣ-ṣifātu 'l-jalāliyyah*), while others are termed the Qualities of Beauty (*aṣ-ṣifātu 'l-jamāliyyah*), and the consideration of this Aspect may help one to understand the Truth that He has no need of any other apart from Himself, that in His Oneness He is Eternally the Self-Sufficient (*aṣ-ṣamad*). In Him as such is to be found the highest meaning of the human pair, represented by Adam and Eve,[34] and of the double symbols, such as the Cross and the Seal of Solomon, together with which may be taken the corresponding elemental pair, fire and water. Indeed fire could not rise, neither could the Cross stand upright, nor could there be anything vertical in the world if it were not for the Extreme Exaltation of the Divine Majesty, just as water could not lie outspread upon the earth, and absolutely nothing horizontal could be found with which to cross the vertical, if it were not for the Extreme Passivity and Fullness of the Divine Beauty. It is in this double Aspect that He is the Creator of the pairs, and it is of Him in this Aspect that each pair is a symbol. Moreover the word pair may be taken to refer not only to two separate things which are the complements of each other, but also to each single entity in so far as it is considered as having two aspects. Indeed everything has an active and a passive asepect: a woman, for example, is passive in relation to her husband and active in relation to her child. The All-Bountiful (al-karīm) is sometimes taken instead of the Beautiful to be the passive Complement of the Majestic, as in His Double Name the Lord of Majesty and Bounty (dhū 'l-jalāli wa 'l-ikrām); but at the same time the All-Bountiful is also active in relation to the All-Capacious (al-wāsiʿ) Who receives His Own Infinite Bounty.

As to the created pairs 'of what they know not', these words must be taken as referring above all to the pairs contained in the different Paradises of the next world. But they may also refer to those pairs of which one term only is accessible to man; for the

34 This highest meaning lies hidden in the Arabic names themselves, since, according to the numerical value of the letters, the combination Adam and Eve (alif, dāl, mīm, wāw, hā, wāw, alif) adds up to 66 ($1+4+40+6+8+6+1$), which is the number of Allāh ($1+30+30+5$). According to the Science of Letters (ʿilmu 'l-ḥurūf) no count is made of letters which, though pronounced, are not written, like the second wāw in the name of Eve (Ḥawwā ').

two terms of a pair need not necessarily be on the same level of existence, and one of them may be in this world and the other in the next. In fact this world and the next, represented by the two seas, are themselves just such a pair; so analogously, are the Spirit and the soul, which together make up the Saint with his two natures, heavenly and earthly; and it is first of all in remembrance of him and of other unknown created pairs, just as it is finally and above all in remembrance of their Creator Himself, that the known earthly pairs figure so much in all traditional sciences and arts.

11 The Symbolism of Marriage

Verily We sent it down in the Night of Power. And how canst thou tell the Night of Power? The Night of Power is better than a thousand months. The Angels and the Spirit descend therein from the source of all decrees by the leave of their Lord. Peace it is until the break of dawn. Qur'ān, XCVII.

OF THE 'KNOWN PAIRS', the highest is the human pair, and the union of man and woman is particularly symbolic of mutual harmony, above all between the complementary Aspects of the Truth, this Harmony being expressed in His name 'Peace' (*as-salām*); thus it was that the Prophet said: 'Marriage is half the religion.' In a lower sense, if the human pairs be taken as symbolic of the two natures of the Saint, the difference between him and the fallen man may be expressed by saying that the soul of the Saint is married, whereas that of the fallen man is unmarried. The nature of this marriage is to be understood from the Chapter of Power, which if interpreted with reference to the microcosm may be taken as a hymn of the perfect soul's marriage with the Spirit, the Night of Power being the soul of the Saint, into which alone descends the Spirit with the angelic powers attendant upon it; and in the particular case of the Prophet, the child of this marriage of soul and Spirit was the Qur'ān, just as in another case, where the perfect soul was rep-

resented by the Virgin Mary, the child of the marriage was
Jesus.

When the two terms of a pair are not on the same level of
existence, as in the case of Spirit and soul or Heaven and earth,
it is the higher of the two which is strictly speaking the masculine term. But considering Heaven and the Spirit themselves, it
is rather towards their feminine aspect that the heavenly desires
lean, towards the aspect of beauty, bounty and loving-kindness;
and on the other hand, practically speaking, the traveller is
obliged sometimes to take the point of view that his soul is
active and dynamic in its quest of the Spirit which appears in a
sense to remain passive and static. Also to be considered is the
maternal as well as the paternal aspect of the transcendent
towards that which it transcends.

It follows from all this that certain features of the spiritual
journey may be more truly expressed if the Spirit be represented by the woman, as indeed it must be according to the symbolism of marriage, if the traveller is a man, whence the structure
of numerous ancient legends and stories, such as those of a
prince who wishes to marry a princess and who has to pass
through many adventures and overcome many difficulties
before he is able to do so. Moreover, except where it is made
clear that the desired union symbolizes particularly the attainment of human perfection, the woman may be taken to symbolize not only the Spirit but also and above all the Divine Beauty
Itself. It is especially in view of this highest aspect of woman
that in Arabic stories and lyrics the beloved is often named
Lailā (Night), for the night is above all a symbol of the
Essence's Infinite Perfection of Beauty, just as day is of Its
Absolute Perfection of Majesty; the lover's desire may therefore be taken to represent, beyond the leaning of his soul
towards the light of the Eye of Certainty, his aspiration to the

Truth Itself, since it is only by extinction in This that the traveller may ever become the Consort of His Beloved.

12 The Sun and the Moon

He it is Who hath made the sun a splendour and the moon a light. Qur'ān, x:5.

ONE OF THE PAIRS which figures most in traditional teaching, being equivalent in certain respects to the elemental pair fire-water, is that of the sun and the moon. The crescent has already been mentioned as a symbol of the Saint, with a passive aspect of receptive capacity and an active aspect of kingship. But as one of a pair in relation to the sun the moon is entirely receptive and passive, so that of the two it is the sun which symbolizes the Perfection of Majesty, and the moon the Perfection of Beauty.

We have just seen how day and night have likewise their origin in these two Perfections. But with regard to this same supreme level the luminaries transmit yet another message: the sun is warm and inclusive, whereas the moon is cold and exclusive. When we look at the full moon, it reduces us, as it were, to nothing as symbol of the One Truth, the Object which alone is. In the presence of the sun, on the contrary, we become more real, because it is a manifestation of the Divine Subjective Reality which is the true Self of everything that exists.

Since the connection between light and knowledge holds good at every level, day is a symbol of the next world, which is the world of knowledge, and night is a symbol of this world which is the world of ignorance. The sun with which the day is lit corresponds to the Spirit which lights the next world, and the moon corresponds to the true man,[35] who is the light of this world. But if, instead of the macrocosm, the microcosm be considered, that is, the soul, which also is symbolized by the night, then the moon will represent the Eye of Certainty, which is the light of the true soul. The direct light of the sun, or more particulaly the ray of light which connects the moon with the sun, is thus a symbol of the Intellect, whereas the rays which the moon sends out into the night represent the intellectual intuitons which act as mediators between the moon of the Heart and the darkness of the soul; and just as the rays of moonlight strike upon various material objects which reflect them according to their aptitude, so the intuitions strike upon the faculties of the mind which if they have duly received the doctrine will flash back a light of recognition; and this light means that a purely mental understanding of doctrinal teaching has been transmuted into the Lore of Certainty.

The direct light of the sun is thus a symbol of the knowledge that belongs to the Eye of Certainty, whereas the indirect light of the moon symbolises the Lore of Certainty. Nor is this significance of moonlight in contradiction with that of the moon as symbol of the Eye of Certainty, since the light which makes the moon shine is not lunar but solar, and the moon itself is in day and not in night, whereas the night, that is, the soul, is lit by the moonlight of the Lore of Certainty. It will be seen from this that although the outer world changes to a certain

35 The moon symbolizes the true man not only for his guidance of others but also for his purity; and here is to be found an interpretation of the name *Ṭā Hā*, (one of the secondary names of Muḥammad) which may be taken as referring especially to these two aspects of the Prophet as Moon of the World, in that the letter *Ṭā*, according to the commentary, stands for *aṭ-Ṭāhir*, the Pure, whereas *Hā* stands for *al-Hādī*, the Guide. Moreover these two letters, if given their numerical value, 9 and 5, add up to 14, which is the number of the full moon.

extent from better to worse according to the general degeneration in the soul of man throughout the different ages, it does not
change fundamentally: even today nature still continues to correspond in its essential laws to the true man, in whom the Sun
of the Spirit lights the Moon of the Heart, which in its turn
lights the darkness of the soul. Here is another illustration of
the already quoted proverb, 'the best when corrupted becomes
the worst': for in the hierarchy of existence the macrocosm
ranks lower than the microcosm, and therefore its possibilities
of degeneration are less. Indeed for the traveller the nature of
the outer world may be held as sacred owing to its relative
incorruptibility, for although the Spirit and the Heart be veiled
from him, the sun and the moon are left as remembrancers.
These are two of the *signs upon the horizons*, shown to man in
order to lead him to the Truth:

> *We shall show them Our signs upon the horizons and within*
> *themselves, until it be clear to them that He is the Truth.*
>
> Qur'ān, XLI:53

It is significant that the signs of the macrocosm are mentioned first, and in fact to the traveller they appear before the
corresponding signs of the microcosm, since the recognition of
the signs upon the horizons is part of the Lore of Certainty,
whereas recognition of the signs in oneself means the realization
of much higher degrees of certainty.

It may be asked, with regard to the fallen man, how it is possible to speak of his acquiring the moonlight of the Lore of
Certainty if he have not first the Moon of the Eye of Certainty.
Indeed, it is true, as is shown by the symbolism of light as well
as by that of water, that the Lore can never be independent of
the Eye, and it is impossible for a man to possess any certainty
of the degree of the Lore if he have not also, by intuition, some
certainty of a higher order, even though the Eye itself be veiled

from him. The profane man, for whom the Intellect throws no light at all upon the 'known and wonted' objects of this world, takes these objects for realities which are independent of the next world, and this complete absence of the Lore of Certainty corresponds to the darkest of nights such as receives no glimmer whatsoever from the sky. On the other hand the full presence of the Lore presupposes the full unclouded presence of the inward Moon. But between these two extremes, there are innumerable degrees of the Lore of Certainty which depend upon such intuitive knowledge as is symbolized by the light which comes from the moon just before it rises, or when it is behind clouds.

It must be remembered that the correspondence of symbolism is analogical; in other words it is not between two things of the same kind, but between two things which are at different levels in the hierarchy of existence. Consequently there appears sometimes to be a break in the correspondence, particularly when the symbol and what it symbolizes belong to two entirely different worlds which are subject to different conditions. This is not so in the case of moonlight as a symbol of the Lore of Certainty, for the difference here is between the conditions of the material world, to which moonlight belongs, and those of the world of the soul, to which the Lore belongs. Now this difference is relatively small, since these two worlds make up one world in the ordinary sense, namely this world, so that the symbol and what it symbolizes are subject alike to the general conditions which govern this world. One of these conditions is that of time, so that not only moonlight but also the Lore of Certainty is subject to time. Thus in time the Lore increases in the mind, and this is symbolized by a gradual lessening of the darkness of the night as the moon, before its rising, comes nearer to the Eastern horizon. But here a break appears in the correspondence; for in considering now the moon itself and the Eye of Certainty, it will be seen that the symbol and what it symbol-izes are subject to quite different conditions: the moon, being of this world, is subject to time, whereas the Eye of Certainty, which is of the next world, is not subject to time at all, being above and beyond it. Therefore, although moonrise is a symbol of the acquisition of the Eye of Certainty, the slow ascent of the moon above the horizon and its subsequent increase in bright-ness cannot be taken as an exact illustration of the appearance of the Eye of Certainty in the centre of the soul. There is a lapse of continuity between the Lore and the Eye; the former cannot really be said to lead directly to the latter. The gaining of the Eye implies an escape from time and from the other general conditions that govern this world, these conditions being 'the limits of the earth' which are referred to in the Chapter of the All-Merciful:

> O band of jinn and men, if ye can pass beyond the limits of the Heavens and the earth, then pass! Yet shall ye not pass if ye have not the authority. Qur'ān, LV:33.

Since the traveller has in himself no means of passing even beyond the limits of the earth, let alone the limits of the Heavens, it may be asked what is the authority which will allow him to pass, or, in other words, what is it that can ever cause the Eye of Certainty to open in his Heart? The opening of the Eye is a mystery and a miracle; it can only be brought about by the Mercy of the Merciful (ar-raḥmatu'r-raḥīmiyyah) Which is said to intervene only where there is sufficient inclina-tion towards It.[36] This depends to some extent on the efforts of the traveller; but by themselves these efforts could never bring about the change, since the inclination which they help to pro-

36 On the other hand the Mercy of the All-Merciful (ar-raḥmatu'r-raḥmāniyyah) is said to embrace the whole Universe without any particular selective intervention.

duce is entirely passive in relation to the Mercy. It is significant that in the Qur'ān His Name the Merciful (*ar-raḥīm*) is often placed immediately after His Name the Forgiving (*al-ghafūr*): for it is first of all by operation of the Forgiveness that the erring heavenly desires may return to their rightful place in the traveller's soul, their presence in its centre being that which counts above all in making up the necessary inclination; and then it is by operation of the Mercy of the Merciful that the traveller may pass beyond the limits of the earth.

The momentary withdrawal of the traveller from the conditions of this world is none other than the 'death' through which it is said that the soul of the fallen man must pass, so that a new soul may be born in its place. Such is the meaning of the death and rebirth that are said to distinguish the holy man from other men:

> *Is he who was dead, and whom then We raised to life, setting for him a light whereby he might walk among men, like unto him who is as it were in darkness whence he cannot emerge?*
>
> Qur'ān, VI:122.

This death, whereby the traveller gains possession of the inward Moon, is what the Sufis call 'extinction' (*fanā'*); this first extinction anticipates other greater ones which lead to still higher blessings. Three extinctions, corresponding to different degrees of certainty attained by Abraham, are mentioned in the Qur'ān:

> *Thus did We show unto Abraham the dominion of the Heavens and of the earth that he might be of those possessing certainty. When the night grew dark upon him he beheld a planet, and said: 'This is my Lord'. Then when it set, he said: 'I love not that which setteth.' And when he saw the moon uprising, he said: 'This is my Lord.' Then when it set, he said: 'Unless my Lord lead me, I must needs become one of the folk*

> *who have gone astray.' And when he saw the sun uprising, he said: 'This is my Lord. This is greatest.' Then when it set, he said: 'O my people, verily I am innocent of all that ye set up beside God.'*
> Qur'ān, VI:75-8.

The consciousness of night's darkness is, relatively speaking, an illumination when compared with the previous unconsciousness, and it denotes the beginning of the Lore of Certainty. The vision of the planet which, like the moon, receives light directly from the sun, marks a foretaste of the Eye of Certainty. Such a foretaste, though it brings for the moment direct spiritual knowledge, is only fragmentary and does not last, being called in Arabic a *ḥāl* (state) as distinct from a *maqām* (station), which is the complete realization of a spiritual degree, represented in this case by the rising of the moon, and which cannot be lost except by extinction in higher degrees. Thus the setting of the moon indicates according to the commentary that 'he turned away from its *maqām*, travelling towards the manifestation of the Spirit', whence the prayer for guidance; and the erring folk in question are 'those who stop short at the luminous veils' which hide the Light Itself. It is said in the Chapter of Yā Sīn:

> *And the sun runneth on unto its resting place. Such is the Decree of the Almighty, the All-knowing.* Qur'ān, XXXVI:38.

The commentary is as follows:

> 'The Sun of the Spirit runneth on unto its resting place; and this is the Station of the Truth at the end of the Spirit's journey. Such is the Decree of the Almighty, Who preventeth anything from attaining unto the Presence of His Unity, the Victorious over all by constraining and extinguishing, the All-Knowing Who knoweth the limit of the perfection of every traveller and the end of his journey.'

13 The Seal of Solomon

Verily I am about to make on earth a viceregent.

Qur'ān, II.:30.

ALTHOUGH everything on earth is a more or less direct reflection of a higher reality, it is only the most direct reflections which can be called truly symbolic. Such reflections are of two kinds, things of which the prototypes have been in this world from the very beginning, without owing their existence in any way to the intervention of fallen man, and things of which the prototypes were directly revealed at some later time.

The true symbol is figured in the lower triangle of the Seal of Solomon. But this triangle does not not merely figure it as a direct reflection of the higher truth represented by the upper triangle; it also shows, by its inversion, that the symbol is an inverted reflection. As an example of inversion one may take this world which is inverted in relation to the next which it symbolizes; and a mark of its inversion may be seen at once in the fact that man, who is in this world the viceregent of God, appears last of all things in order of creation. This is expressed in the Seal of Solomon in which the apex of the upper triangle corresponds to the Creator from Whom all things emanate, whereas the apex of the lower one corresponds to man who is the final result to which all creation tends. This general law of inversion might have been inferred from what has already been said about the symbolism of the pairs. It will be remembered that the two terms of a complementary pair need not necessarily be on the same level of existence, and the two seas, representing either Spirit and soul or Heaven and earth, were given as an example of a pair whose terms are at different levels. In this case it may be noticed that the feminine term of the pair is the symbol of the masculine term, for the soul is the reflection of the Spirit, just as earth is of Heaven; and the same is in fact true of all pairs in which one term is lower than the other. The converse is also true, namely that a symbol and what it symbolizes may always be said to form a complementary pair in which the symbol is always the feminine term. It is this passivity in the face of activity, this being feminine in the face of what is masculine, negative in the face of what is positive, which is figured in the Seal of Solomon and which constitutes the inversion of the symbol in relation to what it symbolizes. Inversion may thus be seen as a law on which the harmony of the Universe is based, since from it results the complementary balance and mutual accord between a higher world and a lower world which is its symbol; or rather it may be seen as a law on which the Universe itself is based, since it is only by reason of its inversion, that is as an entirely negative reflection in the face of the Absolute Positive, that the Universe exists at all; and it is the prevalence of this law throughout the whole hierarchy of existence which causes eventually, in the lowest world of all, the reflection of an object in water to be inverted in relation to the object itself.

The highest earthly example of the true symbol is the true man himself; but before going on to consider his nature as illustrated by the lower triangle of the Seal of Solomon, there is yet another aspect of inversion to be explained, and for this purpose the Seal must first of all be considered once more in its highest meaning, that is, as a symbol of the Divine Majesty and Beauty. Among the Qualities of Majesty, Which are represented by the upper triangle, are all Those Which have to do with the

Overwhelming and Irresistible Power of the Truth including the Oneness Itself in so far as It be considered in Its Aspect of Activity,[37] that is, as overwhelming with extinction all else beside It. Thus, when in the Chapter of the Believer a question is asked concerning the Divine Majesty: *Unto Whom on that day belongeth the Kingdom?* the King is immediately identified in the reply: *Unto God, the One, the Irresistible.* (Qur'ān, XL:16)

It is the Extreme Splendour of His Majesty Which makes it impossible for any other to stand beside Him, and on the other hand it is as it were by reason of His incomparability that He is King. In this connection it may be recalled that the upper triangle of the Seal of Solomon, as well as the vertical of the Cross, is a figure of fire, being in fact like a tongue of flame; and to what has already been said of this vertical element as a symbol of the Exaltation of His Majesty, it may be added that fire would be quite unable to burn if it were not also a manifestation of the All-Consuming Onliness, Which the upper triangle symbolizes by its contraction towards the single point of the apex. In the lower triangle, however, the dominating tendency is that of expansion towards the horizontal base, and the horizontal has already been mentioned as manifesting above all the Amplitude of the Divine Beauty. One Aspect of this Amplitude is Riches, Which under the title of Bounty takes the place of Beauty in His Name the Lord of Majesty and Bounty. It may thus be said

37 The Supreme Aspect of the Divine Unity (*al-aḥadiyyah*) is the Essence in Itself, whereas the Oneness (*al-wāḥidiyyah*) is the Essence inasmuch as It is the Sum of all the Qualities. The Oneness may be said to have two Aspects, Singleness (or Wholeness) and Onliness: the creatures reflect It inasmuch as each is a single whole in itself and inasmuch as each is unique. It is thus the Source of all multiplicity (made up of an indefinite number of single entities) and differentiation. In Its Essential Absolute-Infinite Reality It includes both Majesty and Beauty, and Its Oneness is to be related to Majesty in as far as It excludes all plurality at the level of Itself while implying plurality, albeit an illusory one, at lower levels of existence. For further explanations see Titus Burckhardt, *An Introduction to Sufi Doctrine* (Wellingborough, 1976), pp. 60-1.

that whereas an Aspect of His Majesty is in His Singleness and His Onliness, the corresponding Aspect of His Infinite Bounty and Beauty is in the Plurality and Variety of His Qualities. This must be reflected in all the pairs throughout the Universe, and so, in connection with what has already been said about symbolic inversion, it should be added that the symbol, as the feminine term of a pair, must not only be passive and negative in relation to its reality, but it must also have something of plurality and amplitude. This aspect of inversion which takes the form of multiplicity in the face of unity, of analytical expansion in the face of synthetic concentration, is illustrated by the Sufic saying that when the light first came before a mirror, it saw itself reflected in the form of a peacock with tail outspread. The light, with its impenetrable and concentrated whiteness, refers above all to the Secret of the Onliness of His Majesty, Whose Perfect Complement, namely the Full Display[38] of the Infinite Riches and Variety of the Divine Beauty, is symbolized by the peacock. It is indeed thus that the true symbol, in imitation of the Divine Beauty, displays separately one by one the different aspects contained all together in the synthetic unity of what it symbolizes; and for an example of a symbol's fulfilling this function we may return once more to the true man, whose soul, at the presence of the light of the Intellect, amplifies itself outwards from the centre in all directions that it may be large enough to reflect all the realities hidden in the synthesis of the Eye of the Heart. These reflections appear as the virtues which are the ornaments of the true soul, and which, like the eyes in the peacock's tail, and like the higher spiritual realities them-

38 This recalls the saying that in Paradise men will be clothed whereas women will be naked; for if it be taken in its highest sense, that is, as applied to the Gardens of Firdaus, its explanation is to be found in His Names 'The Inwardly Hidden' (*al-bāṭin*), Which, suggesting His Secret, refers to His Perfection of Majesty, and 'The Outwardly Manifest' (*aẓ-ẓāhir*), Which refers to His Perfection of Beauty.

selves, symbolize above all the Divine Names and Qualities. Another example, parallel to this, is to be found in the riches and variety of the outer world itself; and here may be seen the extreme amplitude of the true man compared with other earth-ly creatures, for being the microcosm he corresponds not to any one of them but to the macrocosm which contains them all. They thus correspond to different qualities in his soul, each symbolizing a Divine Quality, whereas his soul symbolizes the Essence Which contains in Itself All the Qualities. Thus the Qur'ān testifies that man is the viceregent of God on earth, as does also the Old Testament in the words: 'God created man in His Own Image'; for it is only in a far more limited sense that other creatures may be considered separately each as a little world in itself symbolizing the Whole Truth.

In like measure with expansive plurality, the other charac-teristics of the true symbol are also especially marked in the true man; for he alone of earthly creatures has direct knowledge of the higher realities, and the knowledge of these realities and of their excellence brings his soul to an extreme of plasticity and passivity in the desire to receive from them as full and pure a reflection as possible. It is this feminine perfection of his soul in its passivity and amplitude which is figured in the upturned base of the lower triangle of the Seal of Solomon.

So far we have considered only the passivity of the symbol in relation to the activity of what it symbolizes. But in the Seal of Solomon are to be found both the aspects which the symbol has in itself, figured in their relation to the two corresponding aspects of the higher reality. Thus if the upper triangle be taken to represent the Divinity, its apex will symbolize the Onliness of His Majesty and its base the Amplitude of His Beauty. The base of the lower triangle will then symbolize as before the amplitude of the true man's soul which is turned in passivity towards Heaven, reflecting the Passive Perfection, and the complement of this passivity, namely his majestic activity which is directed towards his kingdom, the earth, will be symbolized by the down-turned apex. The lower triangle as a whole is thus an image of the perfect human nature.

The active perfection of the true man as King of the Earth is the result of his passive perfection; for in the amplitude of his soul are reflected all the different possibilities of action, and from these he draws his inspiration to choose the one act perfectly suited to the particular circumstances. The fallen man, whose soul does not directly reflect the transcendent archetypes, has not this same possibility of inspiration, and is forced to rely too much on past experience. Thus his actions inevitably bear the traces of previous actions of the same kind, which means that they have a certain uniformity, being prevented by the fetters of habit from varying in proportion to the variation of the circumstances. The true man, on the other hand, has little need for memory of the past, which may be called 'horizontal' memory. He is inspired by 'vertical' memory in the sense of the word *dhikr*, and has the power to bring forth actions according to the process of the creation itself in descent from their spiritual source. Such an action is indeed a new creation specially made to fit particular circumstances, without the need to refer to previous actions, of which in its spontaneity it bears no trace, as if it were the first and only action of its kind. Thus the Onliness of the Divine Majesty finds Its shadow in the uniqueness of the true man's action. But by inversion, whereas the Archetype is the Cause of all passivity and contains in Itself all the different possiblities, the true man's action is the result of passivity and is itself contained among all the different possibilities of action.

To take another example on analogy with the last, if the upper triangle represents the Divinity in the Aspect of Providence, its apex will represent the Divine Free Will, Which is expressed in His Name 'the Determiner' (*al-qādir*). The base will then represent the Passive Aspect of Providence Which is none other than the Mother of the Book (*ummu 'l-kitāb*), the Eternal Book in Which all things are written, and Which from the point of view of the creation may be called the Book of Destiny. Just as Destiny is Passive towards the Free Will Which is Its Cause, the true man is passive in the face of Destiny, and this passivity, represented by the upturned base of the lower triangle, is precisely what is meant by *islām* in the highest sense of the word, that is, not merely submission to the Law—the *islām* which contrasted with faith (*imān*) and spiritual excellence (*iḥsān*)—but fully realized submission, that perfect acceptance of Destiny which is in fact a mark of sainthood, not to be attributed to the fallen man. As to the downturned apex of the lower triangle, it will represent the true man's relative freedom in action as the King of the Earth; and what was true in general of his activity in relation to his passivity is also true of this particular aspect of his activity; for by the law of inversion whereas the Absolute Free Will is entirely Active with regard to Destiny, the true man's relative free will is the result of his passivity in the face of Destiny. By reason of his extreme passivity towards Heaven he is far more free than any other earthly creature; and since this perfect passivity springs from his spiritual knowledge, that is, his vision of the Divine Qualities, one may see here an interpretation of the words of Jesus: 'Get knowledge', for knowledge will make you free'.[39] Indeed, the greater a man's knowledge, the more keenly he senses, beyond the purely human notion of good and evil, the Transcendent Beauty of the Divine Necessity and the harmony of the Universe which is Its shadow, and the more he shows his own relative freedom in giving thanks that everything is as it

39 In their highest sense these words refer to the Absolute Freedom which can only be regained by extinction in the Truth's Knowledge of Itself.

must be, his own destiny included, and in saying with all his soul: 'Praise be to God, the Lord of the worlds!'

It is the true man's relative freedom, the full desire to do what he must do, which brings his activity to its extreme effectiveness; and this spontaneous activity, which in its emanation from unresisting passivity is symbolized by the lower triangle of the Seal of Solomon, is also symbolized by the element water, of which the inverted triangle is a figure; for just as water flows with irresistible penetration into a hollow in the rock, perfectly filling up every crevice down to its minutest detail, even so the true man perfectly fills the hollow of each moment of his life, while in his outlook towards Heaven he remains like a calm and level surface upturned to the sky. Thus it is set down in the Book of the Way and Virtue (Tao-Tê-Ching), revered by the Chinese as the most sacred of their scriptures: 'The highest good is like water',[40] and again: 'The weakest things in the world can overmatch the strongest things in the world. Nothing in the world can be compared with water for its weak and yielding nature; yet in attacking the hard and strong nothing proves better than it.'[41] Water has these qualities because it is a direct reflection in the material world of the virtue of *islām*, which in its extreme passivity is the most penetratingly active of all earthly things.

---

40 *Tao-Tê-Ching*, translated by Ch'u Ta-Kao (London, 1959) chapter 8 .
41 *Ibid*, chapter 78

14 The Tree of the Knowledge of Good and Evil

And come not nigh this tree, for then would ye be
transgressors.   Qur'ān, II:35.

THE QUR'ĀN does not mention the name of the forbidden tree, but in the Old Testament it is named the Tree of the Knowledge of Good and Evil. The fallen man is in fact guided in action by memory of past experience, and from such 'horizontal' memory is derived a general sense of what is desirable in action and what is to be avoided, which is none other than the knowledge of good and evil. But the true man's certainty enables him to go beyond this knowledge and to choose not merely a good action but the perfect action; thus when it is said in the Old Testament that before eating the fruit of the forbidden tree Adam was without the knowledge of good and evil, this does not imply any ignorance in him but on the contrary the possession of a higher knowledge in the synthesis of which the general sense of expediency remained undeveloped.

To save man from becoming subject to the merely human sense of expediency derived from experience, which is the knowledge of good and evil in its lowest form, such knowledge in its highest posssible form was directly revealed in the religions represented by 'the words' which Adam received from his Lord; and since for want of the Eye of Certainty the fallen man inevitably tends to become the slave of habits, the religions meet this necessity by prescribing the regular performance of rites, which become as it were sacred habits. Thus, through the Divine Mercy, the very limitations of the fallen man are made the vehicles of spiritual influence.

Like all else that is a direct reflection of spiritual truth, religion shows distinctly the two aspects figured in the lower triangle of the Seal of Solomon. But, in this, religion is not merely analogous to the true man; it actually is, in a sense, the true man, just as the true man, or more particularly the Prophet, is the incarnation of religion. The higher aspect of religion, corresponding to the passivity of the true man's soul in its outlook towards Heaven, is none other than this same outlook, abstracted from him and perpetuated. This higher aspect is universal and unchanging; in it each religion is necessarily identical with all the others, for with regard to the Divinity only one attitude is permissible, namely that of *islām*[42] (submission): *Verily 'before God religion is submission.* (Qur'ān, III:19) It is thus that the Qur'ān speaks of itself and the Gospel as confirming what was before it, and this inward identity of one religion with the rest is the clearest sign of its orthodoxy. On the other hand, in the formal or outward aspect of religion, the corresponding sign of orthodoxy lies in the extreme difference between the one particular set of outward forms and the others. For just as the true man's action is unique, the characteristic elements of a religion have a spontaneity and originality which give them also a certain uniqueness. The necessity for this outward difference between the religions is affirmed in the Chapter of the Table:

> *For each We have appointed a law and traced out a path, and if God had wished, verily He would have made you one people.*
> Qur'ān, V:48.

---

42 The verb from which this verbal noun comes has as its present participle *muslim* (submitting, that is, practising *islām*).

whereas later in the same chapter these variations are as it were reabsorbed into the universal aspect of religion which is above all particular differences:

> *Verily they that believe, and those who are Jews, and the Sabaeans and the Christians—whosoever believeth in God and the last day and acteth piously—there shall come no fear upon them, neither shall they grieve.* Qur'ān, v:69.

The law of a religion is for a particular place and period, as a torch given to man to guide him on a moonless night; and to meet the fallen man's subjection to the knowledge of the forbidden tree, it makes a distinction between good, which corresponds to the narrow circle of light which it casts, and evil, which corresponds to the outer darkness. But the true man has no need of this torch; for him the circle of light which it casts is merged into one with the outer darkness by the light of the full moon. It is true that his spiritual vision enables him to see far more clearly than others the beauty of the religious laws as manifestations of the Will of Heaven, and thus his submission to them is quite spontaneous. In other words he identifies them with his own certainty, and they become an expression of the Divine Will not only for a period and a people but for a particular moment and individual. But if by exception his certainty were not in accordance with these laws, it would necessarily take precedence over them, and so it is that the 'transgressions' of the true man are 'forgiven in advance'.

> *Verily We have made thee victorious by a manifest victory, that God may forgive thee thy trespasses past and those which are to come.* Qur'ān, XVIII:1.

15 The Narrow Gate

Verily with hardship cometh ease.

Qur'ān, XCIV:5.

THE BREADTH of the triangle's upturned base as a symbol of *islām* corresponds to 'the expansion of the breast' which is so often associated with this virtue in the Qur'ān, as for example:

> *And whomsoever God wisheth to guide, He expandeth his breast unto submission.*   Qur'ān, VI:125.

The same verse continues:

> *And whomsoever He wisheth to lead astray, He contracteth his breast and maketh it narrow as if he were climbing heaven.*

Thus if the lower triangle of the Seal of Solomon be turned so as to point upwards, it may be taken to symbolize the opposite of the Muslim, namely the infidel, for the upward contraction towards the apex will then correspond to the narrowing of the breast of one whose activity is turned upwards against Destiny *as if he were climbing heaven*—a tendency which took visible shape in the outer world with the building of the Tower of Babel—while the down-turned base will indicate passivity and weakness with regard to the world.

It has already been said that compared with the true man the fallen man is scarcely a man at all; but none the less, it is always possible for the fallen man still to be King of the Earth in a relative sense through making himself, by means of rites, a receptacle of spiritual influence, and through knowing, by means of the Lore of Certainty, something of the secret nature and highest meaning of the creatures that are his subjects. These are the essential functions of man. But the infidel is not merely incapable of them; he even does the very opposite, by closing himself to the spiritual influence and by declaring that his supposed subjects have no value higher than their earthly one. Thus he is as unhuman as it is possible for a man to be; he is so stripped of all the essential features of his kind that he may be likened to a bird without wings or to a fish that cannot swim, being in fact the lowest of all creatures, as is affirmed in the already quoted verses of the Chapter of the Fig:

> *Verily We created man in the fairest rectitude. Then cast We him down to be the lowest of the low.*   Qur'ān, XCV:4-5.

The extreme difference between the true man and the infidel may be considered in many different ways. Since the true man is far more conscious of the higher realities than is any other earthly creature, he is far more passive towards them, and far more fully reflective of them. The infidel on the other hand is not merely unconscious of these realities but unlike any other earthly creature he even goes so far as to deny[44] them. Thus, being the least passive towards them, he is the least symbolic thing on earth; and since things only exist in so far as they are symbols, one may say that the infidel is the least real of earthly creatures, being as it were upon the very verge of non-existence. This applies not only to him in himself but to all he produces, since his arts and sciences are based on the supposition that this world is independent and that the things in it, far from being symbols, are themselves the highest realities. It is true that he and his

44 The word *kāfir*, which is usually translated 'infidel', means literally 'denier'.

works must remain symbolic in some degree, since otherwise they could not exist at all; but their symbolism, that is, their power to recall the higher realities, is so slight that they may be likened to barely perceptible shadows which are about to vanish altogether; and in fact when a people reaches a certain degree of infidelity, it and its works always do vanish, as did countless peoples in the past, such as those of Aād and Thamūd and others mentioned in the Qur'ān, and as will the whole of humanity, so it is said, when it reaches its extreme of infidelity under the domination of the Antichrist at the end of the present age, except for a few[45] who are destined to live on into the reign of Christ.

Whereas the true man is always strikingly unique in his earthly aspect, the infidel tends towards uniformity with others of his kind. In fact, what has already been said about the fallen man to contrast him with the true man may be applied to the infidel in an extreme degree. Since he is as remote as possible from any vertical remembrance of spiritual truths, everything about him is as it were borrowed horizontally, and he is thus so lacking in spontaneity and originality that he can scarcely be considered as an entity in himself apart from the general mass of his fellows. He has almost ceased to be the microcosm and has been absorbed by the world about him in which he is simply a representative of the human race in its last phase of corruption and decay. Through this function he appears as the opposite of the true man even with regard to the freedom which he, the infidel, claims to possess above all. For it is precisely through acknowledging that he is not free that the true man has relative freedom in such a high degree. But the infidel, while maintaining

45 It is said that these few, comparable in their destiny to the families of Noah and Lot, will be from among the companions of the Mahdi, and that they are none other than the elect referred to by Christ in his description of the days of destruction before his second coming: 'And if the Lord had not shortened these days no flesh would have been saved; but for the sake of the elect whom He hath chosen He hath shortened the days.'

that he is independent, is the least free of all creatures. It is his destiny to show, through refusing to be a symbol and through bringing himself thus to the edge of nothingness, that man whom he believes to be the highest reality is nothing if not a symbol, and also, through making himself a barrier instead of a mediator between this world and the next, to show by the resulting ruin of this world that far from being self-sufficient it is entirely dependent on the next.

Time, like all else, is necessarily a manifestation of the Lord of Majesty and Bounty, Who is reflected in the two complementary and successive phases through which all that is subject to time must necessarily pass. These are the phases of birth and death, waxing and waning, growth and decay, expansion and contraction. The first of these phases manifests God in His Aspect of Beauty as the All-Bountiful, the Life-Giver (*al-muḥyī*); and so during such a phase any entity, whether it be an individual or a species or the world itself, may be considered as more directly subject to Him in this Aspect. Such is the relationship expressed in the Seal of Solomon, whose lower triangle is thus a figure of creation in its primordial state. But during the complementary phase the entity is more directly subject to the Majestic, Who is the Slayer (*al-mumīt*), bringing about the extinction of all but Himself; and although in the small cycle[46] of his own life the infidel is subject first to one and then to the other of these Aspects, in the much larger cycle of the existence of the humanity to which he belongs he is subject without respite to

46 Each pair of phases makes up a cycle of time, and time is thus made up of countless cycles within cycles. Even the act of breathing constitutes such a cycle, and may be performed as a rite in remembrance of the Lord of Majesty and Bounty: the moment which allows one to breathe in is a manifestation of the Amplitude of the Divine Bounty, and the moment of breathing out manifests the Exaltation of the Divine Majesty. But the inverse of this, from a higher standpoint, is also true: see Martin Lings, *A Sufi Saint of the Twentieth Century* (London, 1971), p.159.

the Divine Majesty in that he is representative of that humanity in its phase of decay.

In the spiritual journey the extinction of the soul is followed by the birth of a new primordial soul on analogy with the renewal of the outer world after the Flood. But the outer world is subject to time and must degenerate once more, whereas the primordial soul is safe from all corruption, for at the extinction of the traveller his soul is absorbed into the Garden of the Heart which is above time; and while in time the Majesty and Beauty are reflected in alternating phases of birth and death, expansion and contraction, each phase counteracting the other, beyond time they are reflected in complementary states which are as it were simultaneous in an everlasting present without past or future. The true soul remains perpetually extinguished in the Garden of the Heart and is perpetually reborn from it; and this perpetual merging of death into birth, which is a denial of death, is the immortality from which the tree and the fountain take their name. The fountain is also called the Fountain of Youth or the Fountain of Life, just as the tree is called the Tree of Life, and this is the life which is referred to by Jesus in the saying: 'Enter ye at the narrow gate; for wide is the gate and broad is the way that leadeth to destruction, and many there are that go thereat; but narrow is the gate and straitened is the way that leadeth unto life, and few there are that find it.' In this connection the up-pointing triangle, which we have just been considering in its application to the infidel, has a benefic sense: if the two triangles of the Seal of Solomon be inverted so that their apexes meet, the resulting figure will represent the two Paradises of the true man; the apex of the lower triangle, which corresponds to the extincton through which alone the traveller may enter the Garden of the Heart, may be taken as a figure of the narrow gate,[47] whose narrowness is none other than the hardship mentioned in the opening quotation: *Verily with hard-*

47 If in its malefic aspect the up-pointing triangle recalls the Tower of Babel,

ship cometh ease. Analogously, if this verse and the figure be
taken at their highest meaning, the hardship and the lower triangle's apex will correspond to the total extinction in the Truth
of Certainty. As at the meeting of the two triangles there is only
one point, so at the traveller's meeting with the Truth there is
only One; and since the point thus symbolizes the Truth's
Oneness, the upward expansion of the upper triangle will symbolize the Infinite Riches of the Truth Which can only be
approached through extreme poverty. Similarly, if the apex of
the upper triangle be taken to represent the Slayer, its upward
expansion will represent the Life-Giver. But since this expansion is not directed towards creation it will represent more particularly Him Who gives Himself Life, that is, the Living (*al-
ḥayy*); and thus the figure is an illustration of the words of
Jesus: 'He that loseth his life for My Sake shall find It'. Let us
quote here also another *ḥadīth qudsī*, one that is attributed to
ʿAlī ibn Abī Ṭālib:

> Who seeketh Me findeth Me
> Who findeth Me knoweth Me.
> Who knoweth Me loveth Me.
> Who loveth Me, him I love.
> Whom I love, him I slay.
> Whom I slay, him must I requite.
> Whom I must requite, Myself am his Requital.

in its benefic aspect it has its equivalents in the Pyramids of Egypt which were
used as places of burial.

16 The Covenant

*Verily they that swear allegiance unto thee swear
it unto none but God. The Hand of God is over
their hands. Therefore whosoever breaketh his oath
breaketh it only unto his soul's hurt, and whosoever keepeth his covenant with God, verily unto
him will He give Immense Reward.*

Qur'ān, XLVIII: 10.

THE FAMILY of true men, Kings of the Earth, has two
branches. One of these is hidden; its members are called the
solitary ones (*afrād*) and their head is *al-Khiḍr*. To the other
branch belong the Saints of the outer world; their chiefs, among
whom are the Prophets, are given the title of *quṭb* (pole),
because it is the function of each to be fixed as a pivot in his generation.

Compared with the members of these two royal lines of
descent, the fallen man is of so low a quality, especially in later
times, that he can scarcely be considered as belonging to the
same species. Imperfections, which were at first mere abnor-
malities, become as it were normal by continual repetition, and
it is as if a new human race had been evolved in the course of the
ages with special characteristics of its own, differing from those
of the original humanity. Thus in the present age, for the fallen
man to start upon the Path in return towards the primordial
state, it is not enough that he should merely desire to do so,
with firm belief in the truth. The change, which was in earlier

times a return to the normal nature of one's species, amounts in later times almost to a change of species; and if the fallen man were left to himself, his aspiration to become the true man would be as vain as would that of a tree to grow fruit of a kind different from its own. Before he can even start upon the Path it is necessary that on to his degenerate human nature there should be grafted something of the ancient royal humanity. This grafting is often represented as an adoption of the fallen man into the family of primordial men, and the novice is sometimes given a new name which corresponds to his true nature and which serves as a reminder to guide him towards it. Without such an adoption the fallen man would be quite unable to overcome the influence of his degenerate ancestry; but by the change he really does acquire a new and primordial ancestry; and thus it is that in legends and old stories the traveller is always represented as being of very noble birth.

As in older religions, the royal line of descent is known in Islam as the chain (*as-silsilah*), and the adoption of the fallen man is described as an attachment to the chain. This attachment is brought about by means of a covenant (*'ahd*) between the fallen man and a representative of the Saints, and it is often symbolized by a joining of hands. Such is the covenant referred to in the opening quotation from the Chapter of the Victory. The same chapter also refers to the first occasion when such a covenant was made by the Prophet with some of his companions, and it is significant that he received them under a tree:

> *God was well pleased with the believers when they swore allegiance unto thee beneath the tree.* Qur'ān, XLVIII: 18.

The spiritual chain of each religion is necessarily a chain of many branches, for a Master may have more than one disciple who becomes qualified to guide others,[48] and the disciples of

48 In this connection see Martin Lings, *The Eleventh Hour* (Cambridge,

each of these may form a separate branch of the chain. In Islam each branch, in that it offers the means of following the Path (*aṭ-ṭarīqah*), is called itself a *ṭarīqah*. Each member of a *ṭarīqah* is as a link in a chain which if it be traced back link by link will be found to have its starting point in the Prophet Muhammad himself. Here lies the higher meaning of the prayers for the family of the Prophet, for his spiritual descendants are indeed his family on a higher plane of relationship than that of bodily descendance.

1987), pp.109-12. See also in general Frithjof Schuon, *Logic and Transcendence* (London, 1985), the chapter entitled 'Nature and Function of the Spiritual Master'.

17 The Caravan of Winter

Hast thou not seen how thy Lord dealt with the masters of the elephant? Did He not turn their plot awry? He sent upon them dense clouds of birds that pelted them with inscribed stones. Thus made He them like greenery eaten down.[49]   Qur'ān, CV.

That the Quraish might be united, united for the caravans of winter and summer. So let them worship the Lord of this house, Who hath fed them against hunger and shielded them from fear.

Qur'ān, CVI

ABRAHAH, ruler of the Yemen, had built a magnificent temple with the intention of making it a new place of pilgrimage. His chief aim in establishing this sanctuary was to divert pilgrims from the sanctuary of the Kaabah which God had established at Mecca. In order to frustrate his plans the Quraish sent a man of their tribe to pollute the new building, whereupon Abrahah, with an elephant in the front rank of his army, set out against Mecca with intent to destroy the Kaabah. The holy house was saved by a miracle: clouds of birds appeared in the sky and

49 The commentary says: 'These two chapters were as one chapter in my father's Qur'ān, and some of the chief among the Companions used to recite them both together in the second part of the sunset prayer.'

killed all the invaders by pelting them with stones, each one of which was inscribed with the name of its destined victim.

The Kaabah is the Heart, and the pilgrims to it are the heavenly desires, the intellectual intuitions, whose rightful place is on the boundary of the Garden of the Heart. Abrahah's plot to entice them away to a counterfeit sanctuary recalls the words addressed to them by Satan when he enticed them away to the counterfeit Tree of Life:

> O Adam, shall I show thee the Tree of Immortality and a kingdom that fadeth not away?   Qur'ān, XX:120.

The Quraish, guardians of the Kaabah and noblest of Arab tribes, are those intuitions which are already at their rightful place, for indeed, without some intellectual light in the centre of the soul, a man would have no initial aspiration towards the Truth.

Every *muslim* is at war with the devil. As regards *those of the right*, however, this warfare is desultory and intermittent, with many armistices and many compromises. Moreover the devil is aware that as fallen men they are already to a certain extent within his grasp, and having by definition no faith in the Divine Mercy, he cannot foresee that they will escape from his clutches in the life to come. But as regards *the foremost* he feels them actually throwing off his domination in the present and they even carry the war into his own territory. The result is a terrible retaliation, and here lies the great danger of the spiritual Path for one who enters upon it without due qualification. Not by human means, but only thanks to the forces of Heaven, can the traveller overcome *the masters of the elephant*. Now the rites act as the vehicles of these forces, provided that the traveller's intention be pure. In the case of one who has entered upon the path through pride or ambition or from any other impure motive, the heavenly forces cannot come to the rites in sufficient power. Such a one cannot help but be defeated, to fall more than ever under the sway of the enemy. But as for him who enters upon the path through love of God in spontaneous aspiration towards His Light, as a plant that turns towards the sun, between such a one and the forces of Heaven there will be no obstacle. They will thus be able to impregnate in all fullness the rites that he performs, making them like the birds which conquered *the masters of the elephant* and which are, in the words of the commentator, 'meditations (*afkār*) and incantations (*adhkār*[50]), white and luminous with the light of the Spirit'.

The Caravan of Winter, when the course of the sun is near to the horizon, is the first stage of the spiritual journey, when the Spirit leans down towards the earth, that under its influence the traveller may attain to the degree of human perfection. This stage is 'horizontal', in that it takes place upon the plane of earthly existence. The rest of the journey is an ascent,[51] and this is the Caravan of Summer, when the sun mounts straight up from its rising towards its zenith in the height of heaven.

The Prophet said: 'Seek lore, even if it be in China'. Now in all parts of the world there are legends and stories in which there lies hidden, beneath a very simple outward form, the deep lore of the mysteries of the two caravans. The form varies according to the particular aspect which it expresses. The Caravan of Winter is sometimes described as a descent underground in search of gold and silver and precious stones; and this treasure, symbolizing the intellectual intuitions, is often said to be in the keeping of diabolically cunning dwarfs whom the traveller has to outwit, or else guarded by terrible monsters

50 Plural of *dhikr*.

51 The Caravans of Winter and Summer correspond respectively to what were called, in the religions of ancient Greece and Rome, the Lesser Mysteries and the Greater Mysteries.

which must be killed before the traveller can win back his stolen possessions. Sometimes the hero receives a mortal wound and, having killed all his enemies, dies imself at the moment of victory; sometimes, as a result of the recovery of his lost treasure, he is at last able to marry a princess whom he has long loved. That the traveller has in himself no means of overcoming the enemy is often indicated by the intervention of a good fairy, and the magic arms which she gives to the hero are the different forms of the *dhikr* which the Master transmits to his disciple. In its aspect of warfare, the Caravan of Winter is none other than the Greater Holy War (*al-jihādu-'l-akbar*) of which the Prophet once spoke on his way back from a battle against the infidels of the outer world: 'We have returned from the Lesser Holy War to the Greater Holy War.'

One symbolism is often reinforced by another. There is a Greek legend in which the Spirit is represented by a beautiful princess named Atalanta who is far fleeter-footed than any man; she will marry no one except him who can outrun her in a race. The traveller, represented here by the Prince Hippomenes, succeeds in performing this apparently imposs-ible feat by means of three golden apples which have been sent him, in answer to his prayers for Divine Help, from the tree which grows in the middle of the Garden of the Hesperides. He throws the apples one by one in front of Atalanta during the race; she, indifferent to all else, stops to pick up the celestial fruits, and the prince outstrips her.

The Caravan of Winter is referred to in the following verse of the Chapter of the Cave:

> *I will not give up until I reach the meeting-place of the two*
> *Seas.*　　　　　　　　　　　　　　Qur'ān, XVIII:60.

This isthmus[52] is the precinct of his mediation between

52 See p.1

Heaven and earth, and therefore the goal of the quest for human perfection. Sometimes the sweet sea, the symbol of Heaven, is replaced by the sky with its fresh-water-carrying clouds, the lost centre being then at the surface of the salt waters of this world. So it is in a Chinese legend[53] which represents the traveller as a fish swimming upwards through these lower waters. When the fish reaches the surface, there descends upon it from the clouds the Spirit in the form of a bird; and the bird and the fish unite together and become a dragon whose wings and scales symbolize the two natures, heavenly and earthly, of the Saint.

It is said in the Chapter of the Cattle:

> *And with Him are the keys of the unmanifest. None but He knoweth them; and He knoweth what is on land and sea; there falleth no leaf without His knowledge, nor any seed in the darkness of the earth, naught filled with sap nor any dry thing, but it is written in the Clear Book.* Qur'ān, VI:59.

Just as the All-knowing reads the Book of Destiny Which is the Perfect Beatitude of His Own Infinite Being, so also the true man, created in His image, must read the relative perfection of his own soul. Therefore, in order to become fully the microcosm, the traveller has first of all to become conscious of all the elements in his soul without exception. In stories such as those in which the traveller is told of as a prince seeking to marry a princess, the obligation of self-knowledge is sometimes represented by a strangely difficult task to be performed before the marriage can take place, such as the counting of the bees in a hive or of the grains of sand on the sea shore. In this aspect of the Caravan of Winter there lies a secondary interpretation of the already quoted utterance of the Prophet: 'Who knoweth

53 See Matgioi, *La Voie Métaphysique*, p. 49.

himself, the same knoweth his Lord,' which might here be translated: 'Who knoweth his soul, the same knoweth his Lord', for it is by coming to know his whole soul that the traveller comes to know his Lord with the Eye of Certainty.

18 The Caravan of Summer

O thou soul which art at peace,
return unto thy Lord, glad in His Gladness!
Enter thou among My slaves!
Enter thou My Paradise!

Qur'ān, LXXXIX:27–30.

THE TITLE OF SLAVE implies extincton, and it is in virtue of this that those who have reached the Garden of the Heart are called the slaves of God; but this title belongs above all to those who are extinguished in the Essence, and it is used in this highest sense in the Chapter of Man, where a distinction is made between the slaves of God and the righteous (*al-abrār*) who have gained perfect righteousness in that they contain in their Hearts the reflections of the Divine Qualities, but who have not yet reached the Truth. These are they who have set foot upon the Ladder of Jacob which is the luminous axis of the whole created Universe, stretching from this world to the lote-tree of the uttermost boundary.

> *Verily the righteous drink of a cup that is flavoured with camphor, flavoured from a fountain whereof drink the slaves of God, gushing it forth in copious draughts.*

Qur'ān, LXXVI:5-6.

The commentary is as follows: '*The righteous* are the happy who have passed beyond the veils of virtuous living and good deeds and who are now veiled with the veils of the Qualities, yet not as stopping short thereat, for their longing reacheth from the World of the Qualities even unto the Fountain of the Essence and to Eternity. These are they who are midway upon the path. They *drink of a cup* of love of the Beauty of the Qualities, yet not this alone, for it is tempered with the delight of the love of the Essence, and this love is none other than the Fountain of *kāfūr* (camphor), the Bestower of the delight that consisteth in the coolness of certainy and in the whiteness of illumination and in gladdening and strengthening the Heart that was consumed with the passion of longing; and indeed the particularity of camphor is that it cooleth and maketh glad and is white. And *kāfūr* is a fountain *whereof drink* a draught undiluted *the slaves of God*. These are His chosen ones, the people of the Solitude of the Essence, their love being of the Fountain of the Essence without the Qualities, inasmuch as they distinguish not between constraint and loving-kindness, pity and harshness, trial, destitution and prosperity, but their love abideth in the face of opposites, and their delights continue amid graces and afflictions, mercy and oppression … And as for the righteous, though they love the Grace-Giver and the Loving-Kind and the Merciful, yet at the Manifestation of the Constrainer and the Trier and the Avenger their love abideth not at all, and their delight is changed into revulsion. *They gush it forth in copious draughts* inasmuch as they, that is, the slaves of God, are themselves the very springs of the Fountain, since here is no duality nor any otherness; else were it not camphor, for the black darkness of the veil of individual selfhood and duality.'

The righteous are again mentioned in the Qur'ān as drinking from a cup which has been flavoured at the Fountain of the Essence, but this time the flavour comes from Tasnīm[54] which is another Aspect of that Fountain:

54 See p.7.

They are given to drink of a pure wine sealed, whose seal is musk—for this let the strivers strive—and its flavour cometh from Tasnīm, a fountain whence drink they that are brought nigh. Qur'ān, LXXXIII:25-28.

Of those who are brought nigh it is said in the Chapter of the Event, in respect of what they drink, that they are not bemused by it (Qur'ān, LVI:19). The commentator says: 'Their discrimination is not lost in drunkenness, neither is their intelligence, nor are their wits submerged. Indeed these are the people of sobriety, who are not veiled by the Essence from the Qualities (as are the slaves of God); else would they be seized with drunkenness and overwhelmed by their condition (*ḥāl*).' Thus, unlike the slaves of God, they that are brought nigh distinguish between the Qualities, and indeed none but they can truly be said to distinguish; for though the righteous make distinction between them, they have not sufficient light to see clearly, in that the Qualities are as veils between them and the Light of the Essence, whereas they that are brought nigh are on the other side of those veils. Thus they alone may be said to see the Extreme Majesty of the Majestic and the Extreme Beauty of the Beautiful, nor is the one hidden by the other as in the case of the righteous, or rather one can no longer speak of anything as 'other' since they have passed beyond all otherness.

What is named Kāfūr in respect of the slaves of God and of their extinction, and of their drunkenness (*sukr*), is named Tasnīm in respect of those who are brought nigh and of Eternity after extinction and of their sobriety (*ṣaḥw*). But they that are brought nigh drink also of Kāfūr and are the slaves of God, and the slaves drink also of Tasnīm and are 'near', and both are the Beloved.

It may be said, then, of the righteous, that whenever their faces are turned towards the Truth in His Unity, their meditations and invocations and intuitions are perfumed with the

Camphor of Kāfūr, and that whenever their faces are turned towards the Truth inasmuch as He is the Eternal Self of all things, in Whom absolutely nothing can be lost, their meditations and invocations and intuitions are perfumed with the Musk of Tasnīm and of Kauthar. Yet as for drinking directly at the Fountain they know that none may drink of Tasnīm who has not first drunk of Kāfūr.

The lack of common measure between the righteous and the Beloved is to be found expressed in the verse from which the Chapter of Light takes its name:

> God is the Light of the Heavens and the earth. The symbol of
> His Light is as a tabernacle wherein is a lamp. The lamp is in
> glass. The glass is as it were a gleaming planet. The lamp is
> kindled from a blessed tree, an olive that is neither of the East
> nor of the West, whose oil well nigh blazeth in splendour even
> though the fire hath not yet touched it. Light upon light!

The tabernacle is the earth, that is, this world or, in respect of the microcosm, the soul, which in itself is dark. The first part of the spiritual journey may be likened to the placing of the lamp, as yet without oil, within the tabernacle. The glass of the lamp, gleaming like a planet with reflected light, is the Heart, and thus the soul is lit with the light of the Eye of Certainty. The second part of the journey may be likened to the filling of the lamp with the oil of benediction, and the blessed olive tree from which the oil is taken is the Spirit itself. It is neither of the East nor of the West in virtue of its centrality and its exaltation, for this olive tree is an aspect of that of which the lote-tree of the uttermost boundary is also an aspect; but in the fruit of both, as in the fruit of the date palm, 'the kernel of the individuality remaineth'. There is now *light upon light*, the light of the oil upon the light of the glass, the light of the Sun of the Spirit upon the light of the Moon of the Heart, and such is the condition of the righteous; but the lamp has yet to be lit.

> *God leadeth to His Light whom He will, and God citeth sym-bols for men, and God of all things hath Knowledge.*
>
> Qur'ān,XXIV:35.

Muhammad: His Life Based on the Earliest Sources

What is Sufism?

Symbol & Archetype: A Study of the Meaning of Existence

The Eleventh Hour: the Spiritual Crisis of the Modern World in the Light of Tradition & Prophecy

Ancient Beliefs and Modern Superstitions

The Secret of Shakespeare

The Quranic Art of Calligraphy and Illumination

A Sufi Saint of the Twentieth Century:
Shaikh Aḥmad al-ʿAlawī

Collected Poems